THE
OF PER

Walter Hilton

Edited by
Halcyon Backhouse

HODDER AND STOUGHTON
LONDON SYDNEY AUCKLAND

British Library Cataloguing in Publication Data

A catalogue record for this book
is available from the British Library.

ISBN 0–340–54493–7

Published by Hodder and Stoughton, a division of Hodder and Stoughton Ltd, Mill Road, Dunton Green, Sevenoaks, Kent TN13 2YA. Editorial Office: 47 Bedford Square, London WC1B 3DP.

Typeset by Watermark, Crostwight Hall, Norfolk NR28 9PA.

Printed in Great Britain by Clays Ltd, St Ives plc

CONTENTS

Editor's Introduction 7

PART I

1 The interior state of the soul 13
2 The active life 15
3 Exercises of the contemplative life 17
4 Part 1 of contemplation 19
5 Part 2 of contemplation 21
6 The lower stage of part 2 of contemplation 23
7 The higher stage of part 2 of contemplation 25
8 Part 3 of contemplation 27
9 Parts 1 and 2 of contemplation compared 29
10 Bodily feelings may be good and evil 31
11 Distinguish between good and evil spiritual experiences 33
12 What a contemplative should do 37
13 How virtue starts and is perfected 39
14 How a soul contemplates 41
15 Using the virtue of humility 43
16 The necessity of a firm faith 51
17 The necessity of a firm intention 55
18 A Summary of Part I 57

PART II

1 The different kinds of prayer 61
2 Meditation 69
3 Desire better gifts from God 77

PART III

1 Know your soul's strength 81
2 How the soul became lost 83
3 Recover your image of the Trinity 89
4 Discover and defeat sin's image 95
5 The first of the deadly sins, pride 99
6 Envy and anger and their branches 107
7 Covetousness 117
8 Eating and drinking and gluttony 121
9 The five windows of the dark image 127
10 Three kinds of people 131
11 Summary 133
12 Your image and Jesus' image 135
13 Forming the image of Christ in you 141
14 Conclusion 143

EDITOR'S INTRODUCTION

Walter Hilton

Walter Hilton, *c.* 1340–1396, is numbered with three other famous English fourteenth-century mystics. Richard Rolle of Hampole, remembered for his *Fire of Love*, Julian of Norwich, remembered for her *Revelations of Divine Love* and the anonymous author of *The Cloud of Unknowing* complete this well-known foursome. (These three titles are all published in the Hodder & Stoughton Christian Classic series.)

Very little is known about the work or personality of Walter Hilton, and even his dates are less than certain. The little that can be discovered about him has to be gleaned from his own writings. He was most probably an Augustinian canon in the Thurgarton Priory, near to Southwell. As such, Hilton would have lived a life somewhere between a secular priest and a monk at this important religious centre in Nottinghamshire. J. W. Clark found the following quotation about the Augustinian rule at the Augustinian Priory at Bamwell, Cambridge: 'The road along which the Canons Regular walk in order to reach the Heavenly Jerusalem is the Rule of the Blessed Augustine. This rule is simple and easy, so that unlearned men and children can walk in it without stumbling. On the other hand it is deep and lofty, so that the wise and strong can find in it matter for abundant and perfect contemplation. An elephant can swim in it, and a lamb can walk in it safely.'

The Scale of Perfection

The Scale of Perfection, or *The Ladder of Perfection,* can lay claim to having the most widespread and enduring influence of all English devotional writings. After circulating by hand for more than a century it was printed for the first time in 1494 by Wynkyn de Worde. It at once became a firm favourite among the English laity.

The timeless themes of *The Scale of Perfection* should enhance the spiritual life of readers from any century. In addition to its devotional emphasis the book includes down-to-earth teaching about Christian morality. However, the main concern of Walter Hilton focuses on the essential requirement of truth in the inner parts and the growth of the hidden, secret spiritual life of the individual. For any sensitive person who has ever experienced being overwhelmed by the seriousness of sin in his or her life this book is balm indeed.

Hilton writes from a profound knowledge of the evil of his own soul. He constantly points his readers to the grace of our Lord Jesus Christ. His use of scripture is most enlightening, and few preachers or religious writers today can match the biblical insight of this fourteenth-century writer.

The contemplative life

The Scale of Perfection is addressed to 'a ghostly sister in Jesus Christ' who was probably a friend of Walter Hilton and perhaps a solitary nun. In essence the book is a practical introduction to the contemplative life, which Hilton divides into three stages.

Stage one is knowing God, which he maintains is mainly acquired through studying the Bible. Stage two is divided into two parts. In the first the contemplative follows in the footsteps of the psalmist. He or she is to 'Taste and see that the Lord is good' (Ps. 34:8). This experience cannot be controlled by the contemplative but is given and withdrawn by Jesus Christ himself. The other part of the second stage of the contemplative life can only be achieved by those who have a clear conscience and a pure heart centred on God. Hilton's model for this is from Ephesians 5:19: 'Speak to one another with psalms, hymns and spiritual songs. Sing and make music in your heart to the Lord.'

Hilton's third stage of contemplation is as far as one can travel in this life. It is knowing and loving God completely. This can only happen when all the evil sins belonging to a person's human nature have been replaced by the image of Christ. This is completed in heaven. Hilton points to 1 Corinthians 6:17 as an example of this: 'He who unites himself with the Lord is one with him in spirit.' The aim of the contemplative life is to be united and married to Christ.

Hilton goes on to explain how a soul can make spiritual progress in this life of contemplation. He anticipated the leaders of the Protestant Reformation with his radical analysis of the condition of fallen human beings. He taught that in their hearts they harboured an evil image in which were imbedded the seven deadly sins: pride, envy, anger, greed, covetousness, lust and laziness. This image has a heart of envy, a back of pride, arms of anger, a stomach of greed and feet of laziness. He carefully explains how different sins should be handled in different ways.

Hilton is much more concerned about the permanent spiritual desires of his readers than with any momentary lapses into sin. He is quick to point out how people flagellate themselves for bodily sins but are unmoved by the spiritually much more serious sins such as pride and envy. He believed that the image of Christ must replace one's dark sinful image if any spiritual progress is to be made. He also believed that the names of the keys that open the doors to the spiritual life in the contemplative are humility and love, which themselves are a gift from our Lord Jesus Christ.

This edition of *The Scale of Perfection* is largely based on an edition of the book published in 1908 by Art and Book Company. A publisher's note from this edition states: 'After the Reformation *The Scale of Perfection* was a favourite book of Father Augustine Baker's, the well-known author of *Sancta Sophia*, and his comments on it are among his MSS. at Downside. In 1659 Father Baker's biographer and editor, Dom Serenus Cressy, O.S.B., published an edition of *The Scale of Perfection* the title page of which claims that "by the changing of some antiquated words it is rendered more intelligible".' Cressy's text has again been used in this present edition, together with a little updating of particular words, in the hope that this six hundred year old Christian classic will continue as one of the most helpful guidebooks to the spiritual life ever written.

Halcyon Backhouse
Crostwight Hall, 1992

PART I

1

THE INTERIOR STATE OF THE SOUL

Spiritual sister in Jesus Christ, I pray that in your calling from the Lord to serve him you may remain content and continue steadfast. Work hard with all the powers of your soul by the grace of Jesus Christ to fulfil the life of holiness into which you have entered. As you have forsaken the world, and have become, as it were, dead to it but alive to our Lord, so too you must let your heart be dead to all earthly loves and fears and turn totally in devotion to our Lord Jesus Christ. For however well-intentioned an outward turning to God may be, without the heart following inwardly, it is simply a copy of true holiness and not the real thing. Any person who makes an outward show of holiness in dress, speech and actions but neglects his or her inner life is just a hopeless creature. They watch the pupil's ways and criticise their faults, thinking themselves something when they are really nothing. So they deceive themselves. You must not do that. Instead, turn your heart, along with your body, towards God alone. Conform yourself to his likeness by meekness, love and other spiritual virtues and then you will be truly turned to God.

I am not saying that your turning to God will immediately bring you virtues just because you leave the world outside your cell. You should not forget the aim of your life behind your enclosure. The reason you are in your cell, physically cut off from the world, is that you might enter your spiritual enclosure more easily. As your body is cut off from conversation with people, so may your heart be cut off from earthly loves and fears.

So that you may enter this life more fully, I shall write down my thoughts for you in this short book in the most helpful way I know.

2

THE ACTIVE LIFE

You must understand that, as St Gregory says, in the church there are two ways in which a Christian is to be saved. One is called *active*, the other *contemplative*. Without one or other no person can be saved. The *active* consists in love and good works, in fulfilling God's commands and the seven works of mercy, both bodily and spiritual, towards our Christian brothers. This life concerns all worldly people who possess worldly riches and goods and chattels to dispose of, as well as those who hold positions of power to govern or care for others (and these may be educated or the uneducated, unspiritual people or spiritual people). Generally, all worldly people are bound to this way of life, according to their talent or ability and as circumstances require. If someone has a great deal of goodness in him, then he has a great deal of good to do. If someone has little goodness in him, then he has less good to do. If, of course, he has no goodness in him, he must have a good will. All this belongs to the active life, whether it is spiritual or physical.

Much of this consists of great physical effort which a person exercises over himself, such as fasting, watchful prayer and other severe penances and self-flagellation for one's former sins. This also includes putting to death lust and sexual longings of the body so that the body becomes malleable and obedient to the will of the Spirit. All these works, however, still belong to the *active* life. They may be very helpful, disposing a person to go on to contemplation, if used wisely.

3

EXERCISES OF THE CONTEMPLATIVE LIFE

The contemplative life consists in perfect love and charity. It is felt inwardly by spiritual virtues and in a true and certain sight and knowledge of God and spiritual matters. This life belongs especially to those who for the love of God forsake worldly riches, honour, adulation and external affairs, and wholly give themselves soul and body to the service of God. They do this by spiritual exercises of the soul. They give themselves to God according to all the knowledge and ability that is in them.

Now then, dear sister, since this is so, that your nature requires you to be contemplative, it is right for you to busy yourself night and day in the hard work of body and spirit, to attain as much as you can of that life. You must achieve this by means which you yourself find most conducive. This is why you belong to an enclosed order. You can give yourself more freely and completely to spiritual exercises. But before I tell you how to achieve this end I shall first tell you a little about what the contemplative life is. Then you will be able to view it clearly and have it as your goal to which all your exercises and work are directed.

4

PART 1 OF CONTEMPLATION

Contemplative life has three parts. The first consists in knowing God. It is concerned with spiritual things acquired through reason and discussion, through teaching and the study of scripture. This does not involve the inner spiritual life. The inner spiritual life is acquired by the special gift of the Holy Spirit. Such spiritual people have a knowledge which is in harmony with their inner spirit.

What I am speaking about belongs to the learned, the great scholars, who through lengthy studies and diligent work in reading the Bible acquire this knowledge, more or less through the abilities of their natural intelligence. This use of reason, of course, God gives to everyone, to a greater or lesser extent.

This knowledge is good and may be called a kind or part of contemplation, in so far as it is a glimpse of truth and a knowledge of spiritual things. Nevertheless it is only a figure or shadow of true *contemplation*. For it has no spiritual experience or taste in God, nor does it have the sweetness which one feels when one is within the great love of God. That is the real well or spring of our Lord to which strangers are not admitted. But the way of knowing that I have just mentioned is common, because it is available without love, and so it is not contemplation. Such knowledge St Paul refers to: 'If I . . . can fathom all mysteries and all knowledge, . . . but have not love, I am nothing' (1 Cor. 13:2).

However, if those who possess such knowledge remain in humility and love, fleeing from worldly and bodily sins with all the strength they have, then for them it is a good way. It is a real movement towards true contemplation if they desire and pray sincerely in the Holy Spirit. Some people who have this knowledge turn it to pride and self-glory, or to the desire of worldly position and status, to covetousness, or to rank or riches, and do not use it humbly to the glory of God and benefit of their fellow Christians. Some fall into heresy or error, or into other obvious sins where they discredit themselves and the holy church. About such knowledge St Paul says: 'Knowledge puffs up, but love builds up' (1 Cor. 8:1). Only this kind of knowledge lifts the heart in pride. However, mix it with love and it turns to edification.

Knowledge of this kind, is mere water, tasteless and cold. If anyone possesses such knowledge humbly, offers it to our Lord and prays for his grace, he will find God's blessing turning their water into wine, as he did for his mother Mary at the wedding celebrations. Our Lord would turn their unsavoury knowledge into true wisdom, and their cold naked reason into spiritual light and burning love, by the gift of the Holy Spirit.

5

PART 2 OF CONTEMPLATION

The second part of *contemplation* lies chiefly in affection, without spiritual light in the understanding of spiritual things. This is common with simple, uneducated people who devote themselves to God. It comes in this way: When a person meditates on God, through the grace of the Holy Spirit, they feel fervent love and experience spiritual fragrance through thinking of Christ's passion, or some of his work on this earth. Or it may come through feeling some reason for great trust in our Lord's goodness and mercy for the forgiveness of sins; or from praising God for the generosity of his good gifts, and his secret judgements and justice which the person has not as yet seen. Or it may be that in prayer he finds all the powers of his soul unite, and the love of his heart is raised above transitory things, aspiring and moving upwards towards God by a fervent longing and spiritual delight. At the same time this person may have no clear perception of spiritual things or any insight into the mysteries or interpretation of scripture. During this time nothing seems more delightful to him than to pray or think about the comfort he discovers there. Although he definitely experiences this comfort he cannot exactly say what it is. It is the gift of God and from it spring many fragrant tears, burning desires, times of mourning and contrition for sin. These purge and clean the heart from all the filth of sin and bring about a wonderful experience of the fragrance of Jesus Christ. The soul becomes obedient and ready to do God's will. It now seems inconsequential to him what becomes of himself so long as God's will is fulfilled in him and through him. Along with this come other such good desires and inspirational thoughts which cannot be recorded. These feelings are not realised without great grace. Whoever has these or other similar feelings is at that point in the love and grace of God. That love, let him know to his comfort, will not be lost or lessened in him except by deadly sin, even though its ardour may abate. This then may be called the second part of *contemplation*. And even within this there are two degrees.

6

THE LOWER STAGE OF PART 2 OF CONTEMPLATION

The lower stage of this feeling may come by grace when people who are active are visited by our Lord. It may come as strongly and fervently as to others who give themselves completely to contemplation and have this gift. But this state of ardour does not always come when one desires it, and it does not last long. It comes and goes as God who gives it intends. So, whoever has this, let him be humble. Let him thank God. Let him keep it a secret, unless it be to his confessor, and let him hold on to it as discreetly and for as long as possible. When it is withdrawn, let him not be daunted or troubled. Instead, let the person ensure that he remains constant in the light of faith and humble hope, patiently waiting until it comes again. This is a small taste of the love of God of which David speaks in the Psalms when he says: 'Taste and see that the Lord is good' (Ps. 34:8).

7

THE HIGHER STAGE OF PART 2 OF CONTEMPLATION

The higher stage of this part of contemplation is only gained by the person who is in complete rest and quiet, both in body and mind. Such a person is one who, by the grace of Jesus and the long labour of body and spirit, has arrived at a rest and quietness of heart and also has a clear conscience. Such people are at the place where nothing is so pleasing to them as to sit still in quietness and to pray constantly to God and to think about our Lord and his name. That is a delight and strength to them. They feel themselves moved and they feed their spirits on God.

In addition to prayers in the name of Jesus, other kinds of prayers, such as the *Our Father*, the *Hail Mary*, hymns and psalms and other prayers and wise sayings of the holy church, all turn into spiritual joy and delightful songs. Through all these they are comforted and strengthened against all sins. They find relief from their physical pain or disease. St Paul speaks of this higher order like this: 'Do not get drunk on wine, which leads to debauchery. Instead, be filled with the Spirit' (Eph. 5:18). The person with this grace must keep himself humble, always longing to enter into a greater knowledge and experience of God. This is to be gained in the third sort of contemplation.

8

PART 3 OF CONTEMPLATION

The third sort of contemplation, which is the highest form of contemplation that can be acquired in this life, consists in both knowing and desiring; that is knowing and perfectly loving God. It begins when a person's soul is first reformed by perfection of virtues to the image of Jesus, and then later, when it pleases God to visit that soul, the person is taken from all earthly and sinful desires, from empty thoughts and imaginings of all creatures. The person is, as it were, ravished and taken up from the bodily senses, where by the grace of the Holy Spirit he is enlightened to see Truth itself, that is God. By his understanding he perceives spiritual things with a soft, sweet, burning love for God. So perfectly does he see, that he is overwhelmed by God's love and the soul becomes at that time one with God, conformed to the image of the Trinity.

The beginning of this contemplation may be felt in this life. The complete perfection of it, however, is reserved until the bliss of heaven. Paul speaks of this conforming to our Lord, of this union, like this: 'He who unites himself with the Lord is one with him in spirit' (1 Cor. 6:17). And surely in this 'oneness' is the marriage between God and soul that shall never be dissolved or broken.

9

PARTS 1 AND 2 OF CONTEMPLATION COMPARED

The second part of contemplation just spoken of may be termed a burning love in *devotion*, and is the lower part. A third part, and higher one, is a burning love in *contemplation*. The former satisfies the bodily senses. The later satisfies the inner spirit. It is more worthy, more spiritual, more wonderful. Indeed it is a tiny foretaste of the vision, or contemplation of heavenly joy which at present is still unclear and partially dark. Later it will be perfected and turn into a clear light and focused sight in the bliss of heaven. Paul says: 'Now we see but a poor reflection . . . ; then we shall see face to face' (1 Cor. 13:12). This is the enlightenment of the understanding of which David speaks in the Psalms: 'If I say, "Surely the darkness will hide me and the light become night around me," even the darkness will not be dark to you; the night will shine like the day, for darkness is as light to you' (Ps. 139:11–12). As is stated in the book of Hebrews: 'Solid food is for the mature, who by constant use have trained themselves to distinguish good from evil' (Heb. 5:14). Milk, however, is for children: 'Anyone who lives on milk, being still an infant, is not acquainted with the teaching about righteousness' (Heb. 5:13).

No one can arrive at this perfection of high contemplation until he is conformed in soul to the likeness of Jesus by perfecting virtue. Nobody can have this at his command. It does not come continually. It only comes when he is visited by God. As far as I can see from the writings of godly people, its duration is short, and one soon returns to a sobriety of bodily feelings. The whole of this work is caused by love.

So, as I understand it, Paul speaks of it like this: 'If we are out of our mind, it is for the sake of God; if we are in our right mind, it is for you. For Christ's love compels us, because we are convinced that one died for all, and therefore all died' (2 Cor. 5:13–14). So, whether we surpass our bodily senses in contemplation or are more sober in our bodily feelings, the love of Christ is the compelling force in this higher part of contemplation. Referring to God, Paul says quite clearly: 'And we, who with unveiled faces all reflect the Lord's glory, are being transformed into his likeness with ever-increasing glory, which comes from the Lord, who is the Spirit' (2 Cor. 3:18). It is as if he were saying of himself and all other such mature people: We are first changed in virtue and have the face of our souls uncovered by the opening of our spiritual eyes, as we look into a mirror and see the heavenly joy shaping us into the image of our Lord. We travel through clarity of faith and clarity of understanding, and through clarity of desire into the bliss of love. St Paul says that all this goes on in the soul through the work of the Spirit of the Lord.

This part of contemplation is a gift from God which he gives to the educated and the uneducated, to men and women, to those who are in positions of authority and to those who are on their own. But this gift is not widespread, it is special. A person who has spent all his life in activity may have this gift, but usually it is reserved as a special favour from God. Only the solitary or contemplative can receive this gift in all its fullness.

10

BODILY FEELINGS MAY BE GOOD AND EVIL

Everything is secondary, however good it may be, in comparison with spiritual virtues and this spiritual knowing and loving of God which accompanies true contemplation. You will gather that visions, revelations, all kinds of physical experiences, dreams and all other bodily sensations which may be spiritual experiences coming through the ear or the eye or the nose, are not true contemplation. Even warm feelings, or any other kind of comforting spiritual experience, are not to be equated with contemplation. All these other spiritual experiences may be good, and may even come from angels. However, they may all equally be counterfeit, brought about by a wicked angel who transfigures himself into an angel of light: 'Satan himself masquerades as an angel of light' (2 Cor. 11:14). Because these experiences may be either good or evil, it is apparent that they are not the best. For take careful note that the devil may, when he is allowed to, deceive you about the same things that good angels bring to you as gifts. Just as the good angel comes with the light, so does the devil. He can do this in the realm of sight as well as in all other senses. The person who knows about these two types of spiritual experience will be able to tell which is good and which is evil. But anyone who has never felt either, or who has only experienced one of them, may easily be deceived.

They are both similar in the way they are felt externally, but they are completely different as they are experienced by one's own spirit. They are, therefore, not to be greatly desired, or entertained lightly, unless the soul by the spirit of discernment can distinguish good from evil, and so not be beguiled. As St John says: 'Dear friends, do not believe every spirit, but test the spirits to see whether they are from God' (1 John 4:1). I will tell you about one way in which you will be able to distinguish good from evil.

11

DISTINGUISH BETWEEN GOOD AND EVIL SPIRITUAL EXPERIENCES

If you see any kind of light or brightness with your physical eye or in your imagination, other than what everyone else sees; or if you hear any pleasant wonderful sounds, or suddenly taste something particularly wonderful, other than what you know is natural; or feel any heat in your chest or any other part of your body; or if a spirit appears in bodily form to you as an angel to comfort you or teach you; or if you experience any such feeling that you know does not come from yourself or any other person, be alert at that moment or immediately after and consider carefully what your heart is saying. If you take pleasure in the vision or the feeling and it draws your mind away from looking at Jesus Christ, and away from spiritual exercises such as prayer and thinking about your own faults, or from the inner desire for virtue and away from your wish for spiritual knowledge and feeling, then the vision or feeling you encountered is suspicious. If the vision or feeling focuses your affection and gaze, your joy and rest, principally on the vision or feeling itself, then it may well come from the enemy. So, however wonderful and enjoyable these experiences may be, do not assent to them. In this way you will rebuff the enemy.

When the enemy sees that a soul will give itself over entirely to a spiritual exercise he is amazingly angry. The enemy hates nothing more than to see a soul in this sinful body who wants to give itself entirely to spiritual knowledge and the love of God. The enemy reflects that he has deliberatly lost this experience, even though he no longer has his sinful body. The enemy is not able to hinder a person by making him openly sin. But he will try to beguile him with bodily sensations which will fill his soul with spiritual pride and a false sense of security. The soul will be drawn into thinking that he has in these physical things a feeling of heavenly joy, and that he is almost in paradise with the delight of his sensations, when, in fact, he is near to the gates of hell. So through pride or presumption he nearly falls into error or heresy, fantasy or some other physical or spiritual mischief.

However, your vision or feeling may not draw your heart from its spiritual exercises, but make you more devout and more fervent in prayer, more wise in thinking about spiritual matters, and even though it takes you by surprise to start with, it nevertheless makes you more spiritually alert later, and increases your love for God and your neighbour as well as humbling yourself in your own eyes. This is the way that you will know that it comes from God. It is being carried out by the presence and action of an angel and comes from the goodness of God. It is for the comfort of simple souls so that they can trust and desire God the more. If this experience comes to spiritually mature people, it is a glimpse of how their bodies will be glorified in heaven. However, I do not know whether any such people live on this earth. It seems to me from reading the story of Mary Magdalene that she had this privilege when she was alone in the cave for thirty years, ministered to by angels who fed her physically and spiritually.

St John speaks in his letter about this way of discerning the work of the spirits: 'Every spirit that does not acknowledge Jesus is not from God' (1 John 4:3). These words are open to various interpretations, and I have given you mine. When a person is united to Jesus his soul's great desire is to know him only. The stronger this desire is, the firmer the bond between Jesus and the soul becomes. The weaker this desire is, the looser the bond between Jesus and the soul becomes. Anything that weakens this desire for Jesus Christ and draws the soul away from concentrating on Jesus Christ is loosening the bonds between the soul and Jesus. Therefore, this must come from the enemy and not from God. But if a spirit, a revelation, or a feeling makes a soul desire Jesus more strongly, quickly binding the soul to Jesus more firmly in love, and opening the eye of the soul to spiritual knowledge more clearly, and also humbling the soul, then you will know that this spirit is from God.

This is how you will learn not to allow your heart to wallow in or take pleasure in any such physical feelings of comfort, no matter how much delight they give. Instead you must think of them as nothing, or of very little significance in comparison with spiritual longings and steadfast thinking on Jesus. You should not give your heart over to these other things.

12

WHAT A CONTEMPLATIVE SHOULD DO

You should always prayerfully and diligently seek a spiritual experience of God. Then you will know God's wisdom, his endless might, his great goodness and his goodness in his creatures. This is contemplation, and beside this there is nothing else. As St Paul says: 'I pray that you, being rooted and established in love, may have power, together with all the saints, to grasp how wide and long and high and deep is the love of Christ' (Eph. 3:17–18). St Paul does not say that you are to experience this through sounds in your ears or tasting something delicious in your mouth, or by any other physical sensation. You are to know and feel with all the saints the endless being of God, the breadth of his wonderful love and goodness, the height of his almighty majesty and the fathomless depths of his wisdom. The contemplative man should be busy meditating on this. In this he will understand all spiritual things. This exercise is the one thing that St Paul longed for: 'One thing I do: Forgetting what is behind and straining towards what is ahead, I press on towards the goal to win the prize for which God has called me heavenwards in Christ Jesus' (Phil. 3:13–14). This is the same as saying: I only long for one thing, that is, that I might forget what is behind and reach forward with all my heart to hold on to my reward of everlasting heavenly bliss. Everything 'behind' belongs to the body, and everything in the future is spiritual. In this way St Paul ignored all bodily things and concentrated on spiritual things.

13

HOW VIRTUE STARTS AND IS PERFECTED

So far I have told you a little about what contemplation is. Now you may have it as your soul's target. Throughout your life you ought to desire to come to any part of it through the grace of our Lord Jesus Christ. This is how the soul conforms to God. This cannot happen until some virtues are perfected and transformed into love. This happens when a person loves virtues just because they are good in themselves. Many people do possess the virtues of humility, patience and love for their neighbours, but only in their minds and wills. They are devoid of any spiritual delight or love in these virtues. Often they are weighted down by a bitter, grudging heaviness as they engage in these virtues. They only do them because of their fear of God. These people hold these virtues in their minds and wills but not in their hearts. These virtues are carried out in love when, through the grace of Jesus and by spiritual and bodily exercises, the light dawns on the mind and love overtakes the will.

He has been gnawing for so long at the shell of the nut that it has now broken so that he feeds on the kernel. By this I mean that the virtues which used to be practised in a heavy spirit are now transformed. They are now a delight and something to be relished. He now takes as much pleasure in humility, patience, purity, sobriety and love as in any other delights. It is true that until these virtues are transformed by love he does not possess the second part of contemplation. But the third part of contemplation he still does not have.

14

HOW A SOUL CONTEMPLATES

Virtues enable us to contemplate. So we need to know how to obtain these virtues. There are three ways in which most people give themselves to contemplation. They are: first, reading holy scripture and good books; second, spiritual meditation; and third, diligent prayer and devotion.

Through meditation you will become acutely aware of your own wretchedness, sinfulness and wickedness. Through meditation you will know all about your own pride, covetousness, greed, laziness, evil sexual desires, envy, anger, hatred, spiritual depression, anger, bitterness and heavy-heartedness. As you look into your heart you will also see that it is full of vanity and is fearful of the body and the world.

All these evil desires bubble to the surface of your heart. They are like water from a well that comes from a polluted spring. They obstruct the vision of your soul so that you never see or clearly feel the love of Jesus Christ. Such hearts need to be made clean from these sins, which happens when you diligently meditate on Christ's humanity. Until you do this you will not have any perfect knowledge of God. Jesus said as much in his gospel: 'Blessed are the pure in heart, for they will see God' (Matt. 5:8). As you meditate you will become aware of the virtues that you need. These virtues are humility, meekness, patience, righteousness, spiritual strength, self-control, purity, sobriety, peace, faith, hope and love. When you meditate you will appreciate how good, lovely and profitable these virtues are. Through prayer you will both desire and receive them. You cannot be a contemplative without this third type of prayer. As Job said: 'You will come to the grave in full vigour' (Job 5:26). So you will end your life full of bodily good deeds and spiritual virtues. This is the way to contemplate.

15

USING THE VIRTUE OF HUMILITY

If you wish to pursue spiritual works and exercises wisely, and to seriously work at them, you have to start at the beginning. There are three things which form the foundation for this: humility, a steadfast faith and a firm will to seek after God.

First, you need to be humble in the following way. You must think of yourself as being unworthy to live with other people and unworthy to serve God alongside God's people. You must feel that you are of no benefit to other Christians and that you lack both the skill and the power to live a life of good works to help your neighbour, as other people are able to. Imagine yourself to be a wretched outcast, viewed as dung by other people, as you live an isolated life, shut up all alone in a house, so that you cannot bring a malign influence on anybody else, as you are so unable to do anything positive for anybody. You need to look even further than this. You are unable to serve our Lord through any bodily good deeds. You are therefore even less able to serve him spiritually with interior spiritual exercises. Remember, our Lord is a spirit: 'The breath of our nostrils, the anointed of the Lord' (Lam. 4:20, AV). The best form of service you can offer him is spiritual service. St John records Jesus' words:

'God is spirit, and his worshippers must worship in spirit and in truth' (John 4:24).

In addition to all this, you are so worldly and blind to spiritual things and even to the condition of your own soul. You have to understand your own spiritual condition if you are ever to come to know God. It is impossible to see how you can ever think that you are worthy to enjoy the contemplative life, which is essentially spiritual. I do not speak to you like this so that you just change your clothes or move from where you live. I speak to you like this so that you feel in your heart your great and actual need for humility. Night and day you must strive to come as close as you can to the state of humility. You have to believe that by the mercy of God it is the best possible state that you could be in, and you must exercise yourself in it. In this life you can never succeed in becoming perfectly humble. However, that should not stop you from seeking to obtain this perfection, in God's mercy, in heaven. This is my own situation. I feel so wretched, frail and worldly. I am so far from realising the true feeling I am talking about. In one sense all I do is cry to God for his mercy and seek after this as best as I am able. I trust that our Lord will make me perfect in heaven. You have to do the same as this, and even better, if God gives you grace.

If you are genuinely humble, you will never be judgemental about other people's behaviour. You will be forced to look at yourself as if only you and God existed in the world. You must view yourself as being more evil and wretched than any other creature that lives. Because of the enormity and large number of your sins and the evil that you feel within yourself you should hardly be able to live with yourself.

This is how you are to see yourself and judge yourself if you are to become genuinely humble. I am telling you the truth. If you want to be very humble, you must regard your own venial sin more seriously than the bigger and more deadly sins in others. This is especially the case for anyone seeking to contemplate. Whatever prevents your soul from knowing God ought to be your biggest burden. Your own venial sins prevent you from experiencing the perfect love of Jesus Christ more than any other person's sins, no matter how great they may be.

Therefore you must hate and condemn yourself more in your heart for your own sins which keep you from seeing God, than condemning other people for their sins. If your heart is cleansed from your own sins, then other people's sins will not affect you. This is what you have to do if you are to find rest here and in heaven. Ask yourself this question every day, just as one of the holy fathers has suggested: What am I? In addition to this, you must not judge anybody.

You will object to this: Is it not a loving act to tell other people about their faults? Is it not a merciful act to admonish others so that they can mend their ways?

Here is my answer to your question. You, and anybody else who is living the contemplative life, should not blame other people for their sins, but just be absorbed in watching over your own soul. The only exception to this is when another person is in such great need that his salvation is at stake.

There are some people who have the authority and responsibility, because of the office they have been appointed to, to judge other people and correct their faults. They do not do this out of a desire or delight to punish them. Rather, they do it for the sake of the other person, for the love of their soul, for the desire for their salvation and out of reverence for God and his Name. People who have not been put in charge of others must still admonish other people for their faults, but they can only do this in love. They should only do this when the sin is deadly and when nobody else can correct them. Unless there is hope that the person being corrected will change, it is best to leave him alone.

We know that this is the right doctrine because of the

way St John lived, who was a *contemplative*, and because of the way St Peter lived, who was an *active* person. When our Lord was with his disciples during the Last Supper he told St John, at St Peter's prompting, that Judas would betray him. Even though St Peter asked St John about this, St John did not tell St Peter anything. St John turned away from St Peter and put his head on Christ's chest and became absorbed through love in contemplating Jesus and his divine secrets. St John was so caught up with this that he forgot both Judas and St Peter. This teaches us how other contemplatives should behave.

From this you learn neither to judge other people nor to nurse grudges in your heart against them. Rather, you should love them, not pick them up on their faults, and be heartily glad that these people can lead an active life in the world. They face trials and temptations which you are unable to enter into from your cell. They go through a great deal of hardship and pain to provide for themselves and other people. Many of them would prefer to serve God, as you do, without having to earn a living. In their work they manage to avoid many of the sins which you would commit if you were in their position. They do many good deeds which you are unable to perform. There is no doubt that many of them live like this. You do not know who they are, so you should respect them all. In your heart you should think of them as being better than you, and should throw yourself in humility at their feet, since you are the most evil person in your own estimation. Never be worried or fearful about giving yourself a lower position than other people, even when you have been given more grace than other people in God's sight. There is great danger in having an inflated view of yourself and considering yourself superior to other people, even if that other person should be the world's worst sinner. As St Luke says: 'Everyone who exalts himself will be humbled, and he who humbles himself will be exalted' (Luke 14:11).

From the beginning you must embrace this kind of

humility. Then you will make progress and become perfectly humble and will acquire the other virtues. Whoever has one virtue possesses all the virtues. The more humble you are, the more loving and patient you will be. The more humble you are, the more you will excel in all the other virtues, even if this is not evident to others. So strive to be humble, keep on being humble. Humility is the first and last of all the virtues.

It is the first virtue in the sense that it is the foundation virtue. As St Augustine said: 'If you try to build a tall house of virtues you must first of all lay a deep foundation of humility.' Humility is the last virtue in the sense that it holds all the other virtues together. As St Gregory said: 'The person who strives for the virtues without being humble is like a person carrying powdery spices in the wind.' If you do good deeds, fast, watch, or anything else, it is of no benefit to you if you do not do them humbly.

If you find that this humility does not spring from your heart as you want it to, no matter how much you try, humble yourself in your will. Reason with yourself, talk to yourself, and pass sentence on yourself that you should be humble. Think of yourself being humble even if you do not feel humble. View yourself as a truly wretched person because you cannot feel yourself to be the person that you actually are. When you do this do not be upset that your body resists you and will not give in to your will. Endure such false feelings in your body and then despise and reprove the feelings. Crush these desires from your heart as if you were being trodden underfoot by other men. By the grace of Jesus Christ, through steadfastly thinking about the humility of his precious humanity, you will stem the flood of rising pride. Then the virtue of humility which only existed in your will will spread to your affections. It is essential that you are humble, either in your will or in your feelings and affections. If you are not humble and you try to lead a contemplative life, you will always stumble along like a blind man. The higher he climbs with bodily penances and other virtues the lower he falls, if he does not possess humility. As St Gregory said: 'The person who cannot completely despise himself has never discovered the humble wisdom of our Lord Jesus Christ.'

How hypocrites and heretics exalt themselves in their hearts because they lack humility

Hypocrites and heretics are humble neither in their wills nor in their feelings. They are cold and dried up in their hearts and emotions because they do not possess this gentle virtue. They are so far from being humble that they believe that they possess humility. They gnaw at the outer, dry bark but never penetrate to the kernel and taste humility for themselves. They may put on an outward show of being humble through the way they dress and through their holy talk and through their modest behaviour. They appear to excel in many bodily and spiritual virtues. But they only pretend to be humble in their wills and hearts. They despise, judge and put down other people who do not follow their teaching. They think of them as fools who lack knowledge, or as people who have been blinded by worldly living. In this way they lift themselves up and in their own eyes are superior to other people. They convince themselves that they are living better lives than other people and that only they possess the truth. They are sure that only they live correctly and experience spiritual feelings because God gives them special grace which is superior to other people's knowledge and feelings. From this view of themselves comes a happiness in their hearts. They worship and praise themselves as if nobody else existed. With their lips they praise and thank God. With their hearts they are like thieves since they steal God's worship and praise and replace it with themselves. Therefore, they are humble in neither will nor affection.

A wretched sinner who falls all day long, and who is sorry about this, does not have humility in his affections but he does have humility in his intention. Heretics and hypocrites have neither. They are in the same state as the Pharisee who went to the temple to pray in our Lord's parable in the gospel. When he arrived to pray he did not ask God for anything because he believed that he did not need anything. He began to thank God and said: 'God, I thank you that I am not like other men – robbers, evildoers, adulterers' (Luke 18:11). He looked around and saw the tax collector. He knew that he was a wretched man from the way he was beating his breast and crying to God for mercy. Then the Pharisee thanked God that he was not like this tax collector, because 'I fast twice a week and give a tenth of all I get' (Luke 18:12). When the Pharisee had finished, our Lord said that he returned home with as much grace as he arrived with – none.

You might ask how the Pharisee went wrong since he did thank God and spoke the truth. I reply that the Pharisee was wrong because, in his heart, he judged and reproved the tax collector, whom God justified. He also did wrong because he only thanked God with his lips. Secretly, in his heart, he took great delight in himself. He was proud about the gifts he had given to God. He was a thief. He gave himself the honour and praise and love which were due to God. This is the true state of heretics and hypocrites. They do not want to pray, and when they do pray they do not humble themselves or acknowldege their wretchedness. Rather, they pretend to thank God and love God with their lips. They do not realise that this is all an act and that they are not united to God because they cannot love God. As the wise man says: 'Praise is unseemly in a sinner's mouth' (Ecclus. 15:9, NJB). Therefore it is profitable for you and me and other wretched people to avoid the state of this Pharisee and his false love of God. We must follow the tax collector. We must be lowly, ask for God's mercy, for the forgiveness of our sins and for the grace to receive spiritual virtues. Then we will be able to thank God and love him with a clean heart and give him proper honour without being false. Through his prophet our Lord asked for this: 'Where will my resting place be?' (Isa. 66:1). God answers his own question: 'This is the one I esteem: he who is humble and contrite in spirit, and trembles at my word' (Isa. 66:3). If, therefore, you want to have the Spirit of God ruling in your heart, have humility and stand in awe of God.

16

THE NECESSITY OF A FIRM FAITH

The second thing you must have is a firm faith in all the tenets of your belief and in the holy church's sacraments. You must believe them steadfastly with all your will and heart. You may have doubts in your heart from the enemy about some of this teaching. You must remain steadfast and not be fearful. You must ignore your own thinking and not allow a discussion to take place in your heart. You must set your own faith squarely on the faith of the holy church and take no notice of your own thinking. Your doubts are not your faith. The faith of the holy church is faith, even if you neither see it nor feel it. Bear your own doubts patiently as a scourge from our Lord through which he will clean your heart and make your faith steadfast. It is also necessary for you to embrace and honour in your heart all the laws and commands made by the prelates and rulers of the church. You must humbly and wholeheartedly assent to their declarations about the Christian faith, about the sacraments and about how Christians should live. You may not understand why certain commands were made. You may think that some of them are unreasonable. You should not criticise them or find fault with them. You should reverence and honour them even if they are not very relevant to you. You should not allow yourself to be critical of these commands under the guise of being holy, as some people do. The least important ordinance or general teaching of the church must not be opposed by you or by the teaching of any other person.

In addition to such faith, you need to have strong hope that you have been selected by our Lord, through his mercy, to be saved as one of his chosen ones. No matter what you hear or see or what kind of temptation attacks you, you must stay with this hope. Even though you regard yourself as a total wretch who deserves to sink into hell, unable to do any good or serve God as you are, you must still cling to this truth and hope, asking for God's mercy, and then everything will be well for you. You must not move from your hope of salvation, even if all the devils of hell were to appear to you in bodily form and tell you, when you were either awake or asleep, that you are not saved. Even if you were told that your salvation was nonsense by every other person in the world, and by all the angels of heaven (if they could do such a thing), you should not believe them. I am telling you all this because some people are so weak that they despair about their own salvation as soon as they entertain any doubts in their hearts. As soon as the enemy or false prophets make the suggestion that they are not saved, or they are not pleasing God, they are persuaded by such words. Even though they have given themselves up to wholly serving God, they fall into heaviness at the slightest suggestion that their salvation is not secure.

That is why it seems to be so necessary for everyone to have a sure trust and hope of salvation. By the grace of God this is possible for people who have made strong resolves to forsake sin, following all their conscience tells them, and not allowing deadly sins to stay with them, but confessing them, and humbly taking part in the sacraments of the church. People who give themselves wholeheartedly to God and fight against venial sins as best they know how, will place their trust and hope in God even more firmly.

On the other hand, it is impossible for the person who deliberately indulges in deadly sin to put their trust in God's salvation. People who do not forsake their sins or genuinely humble themselves before God and the church are not placing their hope in God's salvation.

17

THE NECESSITY OF A FIRM INTENTION

The third foundation principle you need is a firm and complete intention. Your whole will and desire must long to please God. This is love, and without it everything you do collapses. You must work hard to seek out in what ways you can please God, not sparing yourself as you engage in good physical and spiritual exercises. You should put no limit on the time you are prepared to serve God for, or else you will deliberately allow your heart to fall into vain thoughts and idle exercises. Do not imagine that this will help your spiritual health. You should not leave your heart unguarded or stop doing helpful exercises. You should not seek any comfort from your bodily senses or from your inner vain thoughts, as if they existed to entertain and enliven your spirit. I can assure you that you will discover that this is not the case. I am not saying that it is always possible to perform your intentions perfectly, because you will always have to attend to the needs of your body, such as eating and drinking and sleeping and speaking, no matter how much you try to do otherwise. What I am saying is that your will and intention should always be completely exercised in body and in spirit. Never be idle. Always lift up your heart in prayer to God and to heaven, even when you are eating or drinking or doing physical work. If you have this intention, you will be able to do your exercises more quickly and with greater ability. If you allow yourself to fall into any idle occupation, or if you indulge in mindless chatter, your conscience will be pricked. You will find these activities irksome and vain and you will soon turn in your inner thinking to Jesus Christ and some good spiritual exercise.

As far as the body is concerned it is good to use discretion in eating, drinking and sleeping, in all kinds of bodily penance, and in long audible prayers. The same is the case for all bodily feelings, desires, devotions and tears, and during your times of spiritual dryness. Moderation in all these things is the best way to live. However, you are to set no limits to guarding your heart against sin, longing for virtues and the joys of heaven, and having the spiritual knowledge of Jesus Christ. The greater your appetite for these things, the better it is. For you must always hate sin and worldly loves and fears. You must long for virtue and purity without measure. While this is not essential for your salvation, it is true and will be a great blessing to you. If you fulfil this intention fully you will make more progress with your virtues in a single year than you would otherwise in seven years.

18

A SUMMARY OF PART I

I have explained what your goal should be and how you should achieve it. As a foundation you need humility, firm faith and a complete and strong will and purpose. Then your spiritual life can be built up with prayer, meditation and other spiritual virtues.

In addition to this, whatever you do, in prayer, meditation, good deeds or exercises, whether they are good because of God's grace or defective because of your own frailty, do all within the truth of the holy church. Whatever you feel, hear, see, smell, taste, either inwardly through your imagination or outwardly through your body, and whatever you learn through your own mind, bring everything to the realm of humility and the fear of God, and offer it up to God with the fire of desire. I tell you the truth, that this offering will please our Lord Jesus Christ, and the smoke from the sacrificial fire will be fragrant to our Lord.

This is the conclusion: bring everything you see and all your intentions within the truth of the holy church. Break yourself through humility and offer up your heart's desire only to our Lord Jesus, to him and to nobody else. If you do this, I trust, through Christ's grace, you will never be defeated by the enemy. St Paul taught this when he wrote: 'So whether you eat or drink or whatever you do, do it all for the glory of God' (1 Cor. 10:31). Let go of yourself and offer everything to Christ. You do this as you pray and meditate.

PART II

1

THE DIFFERENT KINDS OF PRAYER

Prayer is useful for purifying your heart by destroying sin and encouraging the growth of virtues. You should not tell our Lord your desires in prayer as he already knows what you need. You should so give yourself to prayer that you are a clean jar which can receive the grace which our Lord so freely wishes to give you. You are unable to experience this grace until you are purified by the fire of desire in devout prayer. Prayer does not cause our Lord to give you grace. However, prayer is the means through which the soul receives God's grace.

You will now perhaps want to know how you should pray, what you should focus your thoughts on in prayer, and what are the best kinds of prayer to use.

When you wake up and are ready to pray you must lift up your heart into a prayerful disposition. You have to cut through your worldly and vain thoughts that tend to drag you down as you reflect on your dreams or concentrate on the unnecessary things of the world and the flesh. Stir your heart up so that it can concentrate on some devotion. In your prayer do not set your heart on anything human. All your effort must go into drawing your prayers away from the earth. Your desire needs to be stripped of everything to do with this world so that you can move upwards to

Jesus Christ. You can never see him as he is in his Godhead and you cannot imagine what he must look like. However, through your devotions and through constantly meditating on the humility of his precious humanity you may feel the goodness and grace of his divinity.

You must set your desires and your mind away from all worldly thoughts and lift them up through spiritual power so that they delight in God and in his spiritual presence. Once you have done this, spend a long time in prayer so that you are not thinking about human activities, or, at least, if they do come into your mind you are not troubled by them. If you are able to pray like this you are doing well. Prayer is nothing other than placing the desire of your heart in God's presence by withdrawing it from any worldly thoughts. Prayer is like a fire. The nature of fire is to leave the earthbound world and to rise up into the sky. When the prayers within your heart are set alight with spiritual fire, which is God, they ascend to God himself.

People who talk about this fire of love in prayer do not know much about it. All I can tell you is that it transcends all bodily senses. A soul may have this experience during a time of prayer or devotion. Although the soul is in the body, the soul does not receive this experience through any senses of the body. This fire of love affects the soul as well as the body, which becomes hot on account of the work of the Spirit. However, the fire of love is not a bodily sensation; it is the spiritual desire of the soul. Anybody who has experienced this will not think of this as a riddle. I have explained this in detail because some people are stupid enough to believe that it must be a bodily sensation simply because it is called a fire.

Now I will tell you what I think are the best prayers to use. There are three types of vocal prayer.

The first type of vocal prayer was given by God himself in the *Our Father*. The second type of vocal prayers are those that have been laid down by the holy church, such as Matins, Evensong and Hours. The third type of vocal prayers are those written by godly people as they prayed to our Lord and our Lady and to God's saints.

As far as vocal prayers are concerned, you who belong to a religious order are bound by your rule to say your Breviary. This is very good for you, and you should say it as devoutly as possible. As you pray these prayers from the Breviary you will include the *Our Father*, as well as other prayers. Psalms and hymns exist to kindle your devotion, as do other prayers like the *Our Father* which were inspired by the Holy Spirit. You should not pray them quickly or carelessly, as if you were upset at being bound to recite them. Rather, you should say them more devoutly than any other prayer, as you recall that they are the prayers of the holy church. So shrug off any heavy spirit. By God's grace you are to transform this necessity into a willing delight. Then your other spiritual exercises will not be adversely affected. After this you may use the *Our Father* and other prayers if you wish. Just make sure you keep to the prayers which you derive most spiritual encouragement from.

This kind of vocal prayer is usually most useful to people at the start of their conversion. Such people are still immersed in the evil of the world and unable to think of spiritual thoughts in their meditations, as their souls have not been made clean from their sins. This is why it is so expedient for these people to pray the *Lord's Prayer* and the *Hail Mary* as well as the book of Psalms. New converts are still weakened by sin. It is as if they are not yet able to run in their spiritual lives and need to hold on to the strong staff of the vocal prayers which have been ordained by God and the holy church. As these new converts struggle against the pull of the world they will be lifted up as they hold on to this staff. They will feed on the words of these prayers like children drink milk. These prayers will help to stop them falling into their own vain thoughts. People who humbly pray like this will discover that this is the path of truth.

It is dangerous for new converts to move away from these vocal prayers too soon. They can too easily fall into thinking their own evil thoughts as they engage in meditation. Secret pride is the root cause of this. As soon as they have experienced a small amount of grace they think that they can move on and need no more grace. If only they realised how little grace they had received, in comparison with the amount of grace God wants to give them, then they would be ashamed to speak about the small amount of grace they had received. David speaks about this kind of vocal prayer in the Psalms: 'I cry aloud to the Lord; I lift up my voice to the Lord for mercy' (Ps. 142:1). Notice how the prophet encourages people to pray with their mouths and voices. He says: 'With my voice I cried to God, and with my speech I sought our Lord.'

There is another kind of vocal prayer in addition to the set forms of prayer. A man or a woman prays these prayers, by God's grace, in the middle of their devotions. He addresses God as if God were present with him in his body. He uses words which most suit his inner state, or words which may come into his mind. He confesses his sins and wretchedness, or speaks about the malice of his enemy, or about the goodness and mercy of God. From the depth of his heart he cries out to God to help him, as if he were in dire trouble with his enemies. He speaks as if he was seriously ill and was showing God his ailments, as if God was his doctor. With David he says: 'Deliver me from my enemies, O God; protect me from those who rise up against me' (Ps. 59:1); or: 'O Lord, have mercy on me; heal me, for I have sinned against you' (Ps. 41:4).

At other times he may be so overcome by God's grace, goodness and mercy that his heart is full of praises to God. As David has said: 'Give thanks to the Lord, for he is good. His love endures for ever' (Ps. 136:1).

God is very pleased with these kinds of prayer because they come straight from the heart. They always receive God's special blessing. This is the second part of contemplation, as I have said. Anybody who has this particular gift from God should stay alone for some time and deliberately choose to avoid being with anyone else. He should be alone for as long as he can because the intensity of this gift does not last long. If this grace does last for a long time, it is both painful and pleasurable to the soul. It upsets the body and makes the person look as if he is drunk. Like a sword it pierces the body and puts to death all cravings for evil living. It forces the body to give in to its power, and even the most worldly person is humbled before its cutting edge.

Jeremiah the prophet spoke about this experience: 'His word is in my heart like a fire, a fire shut up in my bones. I am weary of holding it in; indeed, I cannot' (Jer. 20:9). This is how you are to understand these words. Fire exists by consuming everything it comes into contact with. God's fire, his love burning in our hearts, burns up all the worldly desires we have. Jeremiah says that this fire is 'shut up in my bones'. God's fire of love fills the soul. The mind and the will are full of God's grace as bones are full of marrow. This experience is an inner one not an exterior one. However, it is so powerful that it makes the body tremble and quake. The body is so unused to this experience that it becomes 'weary of holding it in', as Jeremiah says. For this reason the Lord withdraws this gift so that the body can relax again. Anybody who prays like this frequently makes more spiritual progress in a short time than he could ever make in a long time using any other kind of prayer. If you pray like this, you are not required to do any other penances as your body will suffer enough through the experience.

The third kind of prayer remains in the heart and is unspoken. It brings great rest and quietness to both the body and the soul. You must have a pure heart if you are to pray like this. It comes after both the body and the soul have worked really hard; or it may come like a sword, as I have already described. Then the soul's desires are focused

focused on God and he praises God without being troubled by temptations. Paul refers to this kind of prayer in this way: 'For if I pray in a tongue, my spirit prays, but my mind is unfruitful. So what shall I do? I will pray with my spirit, but I will also pray with my mind; I will sing with my spirit, but I will also sing with my mind' (1 Cor. 14:14–15). When my spirit agrees that I should pray diligently with my tongue it does me good, but my soul is not feeding on spiritual fruit that comes from the understanding. St Paul asks what we should do about this. His answer is that we should pray using the desires of our spirits and that we should also pray using our inner spirit. Then our inner being is fed by the sight and love of God. This is how I understand St Paul to have prayed.

In the holy Bible our Lord speaks in the following way when he refers to prayer: 'The fire on the altar must be kept burning; it must not go out. Every morning the priest is to add firewood and arrange the burnt offering on the fire and burn the fat of the fellowship offerings on it. The fire must be kept burning on the altar continuously; it must not go out' (Lev. 6:12–13). So we learn that the fire of love burns continuously in the soul of devout men and women, which represents God's altar. The priest putting on firewood to keep the fire burning stands for the pure thoughts and fervent desires which are nourished by holy psalms so that the fire of love in his heart is never extinguished. To some of his servants the Lord gives this type of restful and quiet prayer as a reward for all their work and as a foretaste of the delights of heaven.

What to do when troubled with bad thoughts in prayer

You may accuse me of exalting this type of prayer to too high a level. It is easy to write about it, but it is very difficult to master in practice.

You say that you find many vain thoughts come into your mind as you try and raise your thoughts to God in prayer. Your mind is full of thoughts about your own affairs or the affairs of other people. You are not able to concentrate on your praying. The more you try to do this the harder you find it, until you feel that there is no point in trying to pray at all.

When you say that I exalt prayer to too high a level I agree with you that it is easier to speak about this kind of praying than to put it into practice. But I spoke about it so that you may know how you should pray. When we fail to pray in this way we should acknowledge our weakness and humbly ask for God to have mercy on us. This is what our Lord himself commanded us: 'Love the Lord your God with all your heart and with all your soul and with all your strength and with all your mind' (Luke 10:27). Nobody can manage to do this completely. However, our Lord has commanded us to do this. St Bernard says that the reason for this is so that we should become aware of our own feebleness and then humbly cry out for mercy, which we will then receive. I will, however, teach you, as well as I can, what you should do.

As you begin to pray, determine that you are going to serve God in this way with all the strength of your soul. Then start to pray, and do so as well as you can. No matter how much you fail to achieve your intentions, do not become fearful or angry with yourself, or impatient with God, just because he does not give you the spiritual joy that you believe others derive from their devotions. Bear your own weakness patiently. Humbly recognise it for what it is: feebleness, which is of no value to you. Trust that through the Lord's mercy your weakness may become more useful to you than you ever imagined. You know full well that you have performed your duty and that you will be rewarded for this, as well as for any other charitable work you have done, even though you have not achieved your intentions. So do what you are able to do, allow our

Lord to give you what he decides, and do not try to teach God what he should be doing. View yourself as a wretch who is culpable for behaving like this. At the same time remember that this fault of yours, along with all your other venial sins, which you are unable to conquer in this life, directs your heart to God. Do not become defeated by your weakness. Instead, acknowledge your wretchedness, call out for God to have mercy on you and to forgive you, and resolve to do better next time. Even if you should fall in the same way again, or a hundred times, or a thousand times, just do as I have told you and you will be all right. The soul that is troubled by these thoughts in prayer can be made humble in everything else she does in life, so that she will have a great reward in heaven for all her good intentions and endeavours.

2

MEDITATION

You must understand that in meditation there is no such thing as a single rule which everybody must follow. Progress in meditation is a gift from God. As we keep on meditating, and as we continue in our virtues, God enables us to advance in meditation and in our knowledge of and love for him. People who do not make progress in meditation are hardly increasing their love for God. This is seen in the way that the apostles were filled with the burning love of the Holy Spirit at Pentecost. They did not become foolish people but very wise people. They spoke about God and experienced spiritual sensations. As the Bible says: 'All of them were filled with the Holy Spirit and began to speak in other tongues as the Spirit enabled them' (Acts 2:4). As they were overcome by God's love they became wise through the work of the Holy Spirit in them.

The Lord places various kinds of meditations in a person's heart. I mention some of these now so that you may experience them for yourself. After a person has been converted, much of his thinking is preoccupied with his worldly sins which weigh down his heart. With many tears he humbly asks God to forgive him and have mercy on him. If his conscience is deeply touched about his sins our

Lord will soon forgive him his sins. However, this person's sins will be constantly before him and they will seem to be so horrible that he cannot bear their sight. Even though he does confess his sins to God he will still feel guilty, as if he had not confessed them properly. He can hardly rest, and he would not be able to endure this experience if our Lord did not comfort him with thoughts about his passion. In his mercy, God not only forgives sins now, he also forgives the sins so that no pain will have to be endured in purgatory for them. We only have to bear the pain of remorse in our consciences now. Everybody must experience the purging of his sins before he can receive God's love. David often speaks about this spiritual exercise in the Psalms: 'Have mercy on me, O God, according to your unfailing love' (Ps. 51:1).

During this spiritual exercise, or after it, our Lord gives him a meditation on his humanity, or his birth, or his passion and the comfort of our Lady, St Mary. This gift is bestowed both on people who are preoccupied with their sins and on those who are living innocent lives. The Holy Spirit gives this spiritually worthwhile meditation to you. You will know that you have received this meditation when your mind is suddenly taken away from all worldly activity as your soul sees the Lord Jesus as he was on this earth. You will view the Lord Jesus as he is taken by the Jews and tied up like a thief, beaten, mocked, scourged and condemned to die. You see him carrying his cross on his own back and then being cruelly nailed to this cross. You see the crown of thorns on his head and the spear piercing his heart. Your heart is stirred with great compassion for your Lord Jesus. You cry and mourn. Your whole body and soul cries out in wonder at his goodness, love, patience and humility. You are overwhelmed that he should go through all this pain for a sinner like you. But you see him so full of goodness and mercy that you take heart and you express your own love and joy and happiness in your Lord Jesus. You shed many happy tears as you realise that your sins are forgiven and that you now enjoy the salvation of your soul because of your Lord's precious passion. So whenever you experience our Lord's passion, or any other part of his humanity, remember that this is not the result of your own work, but comes from the grace of the Holy Spirit. When the spiritual eyes catch a glimpse of the humanity of Christ like this they are, as St Bernard said, focusing on the human love of God. This is beneficial in destroying important sins. A good route to approach the virtues is to contemplate the Godhead. Nobody can contemplate Christ as God who has not agonised in his mind over his humanity.

This was the case with St Paul. First of all he 'resolved to know nothing while I was with you except Jesus Christ and him crucified' (1 Cor. 2:2). It is as if he said that his faith came only from the passion of Christ. So he also said: 'May I never boast except in the cross of our Lord Jesus Christ' (Gal. 6:14). However, he did say later on: 'We preach Christ crucified: a stumbling-block to Jews and foolishness to Gentiles, but to those whom God has called, both Jews and Greeks, Christ the power of God and the wisdom of God' (1 Cor. 1:23–24). Paul is saying that he started by preaching about the humanity of the passion of Christ and then went on to preach about the divinity of Christ, that is Christ as the power and wisdom of God.

You cannot meditate like this at will, but only when our Lord gives you this gift. Some people receive this gift spasmodically throughout their lives. Some people are so sensitive in their spiritual lives that they only have to hear other people referring to Christ's passion and they are comforted in their struggle against temptation. Some other people receive this meditation soon after their conversion, but then the divine gift is withdrawn. This prevents these people becoming proud in their own sight. Sometimes the divine gift is taken away because of one particular sin, while at other times it may be withdrawn so that these people can become stronger spiritually as they fight against temptation. After this they appreciate the close presence of our Lord even more. Jesus said to his disciples: 'It is for your good that I am going away' (John 16:7). While Jesus was with his disciples they loved him greatly, but only as a human being. Our Lord had to take his bodily presence away from them so that the Holy Spirit could come to them. Then the Holy Spirit would be able to teach the disciples how to love and know our Lord in a more spiritual way. This happened at Pentecost. In the same way, it is expedient that our Lord should withdraw himself from some people so that their hearts can be more set on seeking him in a spiritual way.

The enemy's temptations and how to beat them

Once people are deprived of our Lord's spiritual strength they may fall into temptations from the enemy. The enemy realises how open they are to attack as soon as devotion has been withdrawn from them. They are left exposed to the temptations of lust and gluttony. They feel the temptations even more strongly than when they readily gave themselves over to such sins. They believe that it is impossible to withstand such attacks for long. Therefore, they long for their previous comfort and dread falling away from God into such public sins. God allows the devil to make them want to turn away from their good intentions and return to their former way of living. Anybody who withstands a little pain and who stays with God and does not return to his sins will discover that the hand of the Lord is close to him. Although the person will be unaware of it himself, our Lord will help him quickly as he has a genuine concern for him. As David said in the person of our Lord: 'I will be with him in trouble, I will deliver him and honour him' (Ps. 91:15). With malice the devil tempts people into spiritual sins, such as doubting articles of belief or doubting the sacrament of our Lord's body. They may also be tempted to despair, to blaspheme against God or one of his saints, to become bitter towards others or even to damage their own health by giving themselves too much in the service of God. People who live alone may be frightened by seeing horrific shapes in their imagination. This may become so acute that they shake and quake whether they are asleep or awake. The enemy uses many other ways to tempt which I cannot go into now.

Here are the answers to these temptations. First of all you must put all your trust in the Lord Jesus Christ. Think about his passion and the suffering he went through for us. Then you can view all your sufferings in a positive way since through them you can be cleansed from your previous sins. So long as you stand firm and do not deliberately turn back to sin in these sufferings, you will discover that they bring you more of God's grace.

Another way to defeat these temptations is not to be afraid of them. Do not equate the temptation to despair or blaspheme or doubt the sacraments with the sin of despair or blasphemy or doubting the sacraments. Going through these temptations does not defile the soul any more than if your soul should hear a hound bark or feel a flea biting. They irritate the soul but they do not damage it. You must despise temptation and not give it a place of unwarranted importance in your life. The more you become preoccupied with the temptation the more likely you are to give in to it. Keep your minds away from the temptations and concentrate on living your life. If temptations still will not go away, do not become upset or heavy in your spirit. Out of your love for God put up with the temptation as you place your trust in God. Temptations are like other sicknesses which attack the body. They may be allowed by our Lord so that we have our sins cleansed by them. Jesus was prepared to be whipped and die on the cross out of his love for us.

It is also a good idea to confide about these temptations, at their inception, with a wise counsellor. Then the temptations will not be allowed to take root in your heart and you will be forced to follow somebody else's advice in this matter. But do not share your temptations with a worldly man, who is not troubled with such temptations, because he may just make your soul despair.

Here is the remedy for the kind of temptation which suggests that God has left you, when, in fact, he has not. The Lord said to his prophet Isaiah: 'For a brief moment I abandoned you, but with deep compassion I will bring you back. In a surge of anger I hid my face from you for a moment, but with everlasting kindness I will have compassion on you' (Isa. 54:7–8). It is as if he says: I have allowed you to suffer for a time and I have hurt you in my wrath. The pain and the penance you suffer now is like a pinprick in comparison with the pain of hell or purgatory. God says: In my great mercy I will come to you when you think that everything is lost. As Job said: 'Life will be brighter than noonday, and darkness will become like morning' (Job 11:17). So when you feel like giving up because you are so depressed by temptations, you are to exercise strong faith in God and you are to pray to God. Then life will be brighter than noonday. Your heart will rejoice in your firm trust in God.

The writer of Ecclesiasticus comforts people who may despair in their temptations like this: 'Though she takes him at first through winding ways, bringing fear and faintness on him, trying him out with her discipline till she can trust him, and testing him with her ordeals, she then comes back to him on the straight road, makes him happy and reveals her secrets to him' (Ecclus. 4:17–18, NJB). To prevent people from despairing in temptation the wise man says: In temptation our Lord does not desert a person but goes with him from the start to the finish. In the first place the Lord chooses him when he draws him through the encouragement of the devotion. Then the Lord brings him sadness and trials when he withdraws the devotion and allows him to be tempted. The Lord tests him with these trials until the person fully puts his trust in the Lord. Then the Lord leads the person in the paths of righteousness, revealing his secrets to him, and giving him the riches of knowing and understanding God's righteousness.

In the light of this you can see how useful temptations can

be. Even though they are upsetting they enable you to forsake your sin so long as you are prepared to do God's will and not revert to your original sins, no matter how painful the temptation is. Stand firm and pray with hope. Our Lord, in his boundless goodness, has pity on his creatures, and in good time will stop the devil from attacking you. Then the darkness of the soul will be replaced by the light of God's grace. He will understand the purpose behind all this suffering and will be given fresh strength to withstand the enemy and all deadly sins with ease. He will be led into a virtuous and good life which he will stay in so long as he remains humble. I have gone through all this with you so that you may not fear temptation and so that through the grace of Jesus Christ you may always be able to overcome your enemy.

After you have escaped from these temptations, or after the Lord has protected you from being tempted, beware that you do not lapse into idleness. Too many people presume that they are ready to rest in contemplation because they relax too quickly. You should at once start something new, meditation. Come to understand what meditation is, and through meditation come to a spiritual understanding of God. As St Augustine has said: 'Through knowing myself I come to an understanding of God.' This is not an obligatory exercise unless you feel that God's grace is directing you this way. For our Lord has given different gifts to different people. No one person possesses all God's gifts, and love is the only gift that is given to everyone.

So if God has given you a gift, such as devotion in prayer or meditating on the passion of Christ, do not become bored with it. Treasure it and use it fully and desire an even better gift which God will give you. If your present gift is taken away and you perceive a greater gift, then pursue the latter in favour of the former.

3

DESIRE BETTER GIFTS FROM GOD

Our holy fathers taught us that we should know the extent of our gift and exercise it and not presume that we have more than we have in reality. We may always long for the best, but we may not always be able to exercise the best if we have not yet received it. If a hound only chases a hare because the other hounds are doing this, he will quickly become weary and will give up and go home. But if he has seen the hare for himself he will be eager to give chase until he has caught the hare, no matter how tired he may be. The same is true in the spiritual realm. If a person neglects the gift that God has given him, and runs after another gift that God has not given him, just because he has read about it or seen it in someone else's life, he will quickly tire of this pursuit. But if he continues to use his gift faithfully and humbly he will run well. So desire as much as you wish from God, because the more you desire from God the more you will receive. Work as hard as you can, and always ask for God's mercy. This is what St Paul taught: 'Each man has his own gift from God; one has this gift, another has that' (1 Cor. 7:7); 'To each one of us grace has been given as Christ apportioned it' (Eph. 4:7); 'There are different kinds of gifts, but the same Spirit' (1 Cor. 12:4); 'To one there is given through the Spirit the message of wisdom, to another the message of knowledge by means of the same Spirit' (1 Cor. 12:8). St Paul says that everyone has been given a gift from God: 'We have not received the spirit of the world but the Spirit who is from God, that we may understand what God has freely given us' (1 Cor. 2:12). So it is important that we know what gifts God has given us because it is through them that we shall be saved. Some are saved by bodily deed, some by acts of mercy, some by penance, some through mourning for their sins, while others are saved through preaching and teaching.

PART III

1

KNOW YOUR SOUL'S STRENGTH

There is one more way to enter into contemplation. You must know yourself, your own soul and its strength.

From this inner view you will see the natural dignity it possessed when it was first created. You will also see the wretchedness of the sin you have fallen into. This will inspire you to recover your original dignity and greatness. You will loathe yourself and want to destroy everything that prevents you from regaining your dignity. This is hard, spiritual work. It is painful to start with, for anybody who sets about it seriously. The soul has to battle against the fundamental sin of man placing trust in himself. St Augustine says that out of this misplaced love of self all kinds of venial and deadly sins come.

This ground has to be broken up and deeply dug over before worldly loves and fears can be uprooted. A soul is unable to feel the burning love of Jesus Christ or experience his gracious presence or have a clear view of spiritual things until the ground has been cleared. So you must work hard to draw your heart away from its worldly longings and love of self until it is totally dissatisfied with itself. Then the soul will be weary and feel pain because it is not resting in the love of Jesus.

This work is very painful and the route is very narrow

for all who wish to travel this way. As Christ taught in the gospel: 'Make every effort to enter through the narrow door, because many, I tell you, will try to enter and will not be able to' (Luke 13:24). Just how narrow this way is Christ teaches in another place: 'Small is the gate and narrow the road that leads to life, and only a few find it' (Matt. 7:14). So, says Christ: 'If anyone would come after me, he must deny himself and take up his cross and follow me' (Matt. 16:24); 'The man who loves his life will lose it, while the man who hates his life in this world will keep it for eternal life' (John 12:25). So for the love of Christ you must forsake all worldly desires and delights. To take up Christ's cross means to suffer the pain that is involved in contemplating his humanity and divinity. This is a straight and narrow way which no bodily thing can pass through, as it kills all sin. As St Paul says: 'Put to death, therefore, whatever belongs to your earthly nature' (Col. 3:5). He is not talking about our body, but our soul. 'Put to death . . . sexual immorality, impurity, lust, evil desires and greed' (Col. 3:5). Up to now you have been trying to resist temptations that attack your body. Now, in your spiritual work, you must destroy the foundation of sin in yourself as well as you can. So that you can do this I will advise you as much as I am able.

2

HOW THE SOUL BECAME LOST

Man's soul comprises three parts: the mind, the understanding and the will. It reflects the divine Trinity in the following ways. Through the mind, God the Father has enabled men and women to have a continual awareness of God. The soul's understanding mirrors the infinite wisdom of the Son, as it was created perfectly clear and bright, without any error or darkness. Man's will and emotions were created pure and clean and were on fire with love for God. The soul did not have any sensual love of the body because of the sovereign goodness of God the Holy Spirit. So it is like the Holy Spirit in this respect, because the Holy Spirit is love. So a man's soul, which can be seen as a created trinity, was originally made with its three parts, all of which reflect the uncreated Trinity, who is God.

This was the dignity and position of the first soul. But when Adam sinned and chose to delight in himself and in the creatures, he lost his dignity and exchanged his godly trinity for a dark and wretched trinity. He forgot God and deliberately indulged in loving himself. As David says in the Psalms: 'A man who has riches without understanding is like the beasts that perish' (Ps. 49:20).

Observe the wretchedness of your soul. Your mind

started by being focused on God, but has now forgotten him and seeks pleasure in one creature after another. Your soul never enjoys real rest, which can only be found in God. It is the same with the understanding and the will and the emotions. They were spiritual and pure, but now indulge themselves in lust, gluttony and pride. Their spiritual appetite has vanished and they have no love for God in their hearts.

Everybody who lives in the spirit understands all this completely. Because of the first man's sin this is the soul's wretched condition besides all the other sins you have deliberately added to this. Through this first sin was lost the righteousness in which we were created. So even if you had never committed any sins yourself, you would not have been saved if our Lord Jesus Christ's precious passion had not rescued and restored you.

If I have been speaking on a plane that is too high for you, I will now come down to your level, so that we may both benefit from this. Even if you were not a wretch and had never sinned, you must now deny yourself and forget all your deeds, the good ones and the bad ones, and cry to God for mercy. Ask God to save you through Christ's precious passion, in which you must place your trust. Then you will undoubtedly receive God's forgiveness. You will be saved from every sin, including original sin. You will be as safe as an enclosed anchoress. Anyone can enter into this experience of God's forgiveness. Even if someone has been a sinner all their lives, they too can submit themselves to the sacraments of the holy church and ask for God's mercy through the merits of this precious passion of our Lord Jesus Christ, and they will be safe and come to the joy of heaven.

Even though you know this, I delight in speaking to you about it. Then you will view our Lord's everlasting mercy and see how low he has stooped for you and me and for all other sinners. This is what the prophet says in the person of our Lord: 'And everyone who calls on the name of the

Lord will be saved' (Joel 2:32). This refers to anybody asking to be saved through Jesus and his passion.

Some people understand our Lord's generosity and are therefore saved. Others trust in God's mercy and our Lord's generosity but decide to stay in their sins. They think that they will derive some benefit from doing this, but they are wrong and only damn themselves.

You may object to this and point out that some religious books seem to teach that some people are unable to love the name of Jesus and do not experience spiritual joy and so will never reach heaven. I too have read these books, and they fill me with fear. I hope that through the mercy of our Lord such people will be kept safe, as they keep the commandments and repent of their former evil lives, even though they never previously experienced the spiritual delights found in the name of Jesus. I am amazed that they should say otherwise.

I think what they are saying is true and does not contradict what I am saying. The name of Jesus in English means 'healer' or 'health'. Every person who is alive is spiritually sick. Nobody lives without sin. As St John said about himself and about other spiritually advanced people: 'If we claim to be without sin, we deceive ourselves and the truth is not in us. If we confess our sins, [God] is faithful and just and will forgive us our sins and purify us from all unrighteousness' (1 John 1:8–9). Nobody can enter into the joy of heaven without first being healed of his spiritual sickness. Nobody can acquire this spiritual healing through using his mind, unless he desires it and longs for it with a loving heart. The name of Jesus is nothing other than spiritual health. So it is true when they say that nobody can be saved unless he loves the name of Jesus. Nobody can be spiritually healed until he loves and longs for spiritual health. It is the same with any bodily illness. An ill person longs, above everything else, to be well again. All the money in the world would not cure him or bring him happiness. It is the same for the person who is spiritually sick and feels the pain of his spiritual illness. He longs for nothing else other than spiritual health which comes from Jesus and without which all the joys of heaven give him no delight. This is why when our Lord became incarnate he would not allow people to call him by his divine name. He could only be called by the name which spoke of the salvation he came to bring to people's souls. So nobody can be saved unless he loves the salvation which only our Lord brings through the merits of his passion. Even a person who lives in the lowest degree of love may experience this divine love.

It is also true that anyone who does not experience spiritual joy from loving Jesus now will be in the same position in heaven. But the person in the lowest degree of love in this life, who keeps God's commandments, will be saved and will receive a great reward in heaven from God. For our Lord has said: 'In my Father's house are many rooms' (John 14:2). Some souls are perfect and are already filled with the love and graces of the Holy Spirit and are able to sing beautifully and lovingly to God in contemplation. These people are called God's special friends. Because they have so much love and grace from the Holy Spirit they also have the highest reward in heaven. Other people do not achieve contemplation and are not mature in their love of God. This was the case with the apostles and martyrs in the early days of the Christian church. They have a lower order in heaven and are called God's friends. This is how our Lord refers to them: 'I will sing for the one I love a song about his vineyard. My loved one had a vineyard on a fertile hillside' (Isa. 5:1). It is as if he said: You are my friends because you have kept my commandments and have preferred my love to the love of the world. You have loved me more than anything on earth, and so you will feed on the spiritual food of the bread of life. But those of you who are my special friends have done more than just keep my commands. Of your own free will you have carried out my wishes and have loved me completely with your souls. You have burned with my love and spiritual delight, as did the apostles and martyrs and all other people who attained to this gift of spiritual maturity through God's grace. You will become drunk with the finest wine from my cellar, which is the supreme joy of love in heaven.

3

RECOVER YOUR IMAGE OF THE TRINITY

Just because we have received God's mercy we are not to be careless about the way we live. The opposite should be the case. Now that we have had our dignity restored through our Lord's passion, which Adam lost, we should be even keener to please our Lord. We cannot fully restore this lost image in this life. We have but a shadow of what we will experience in heaven. We begin this now as we contemplate and open our spiritual eyes to seeing God. This will be perfected in heaven. Our Lord promised this to St Mary Magdalene, a genuine contemplative, when he said: 'Mary has chosen what is better [which is loving God in contemplation], and it will not be taken away from her' (Luke 10:42).

In this life you will never recover the perfect innocence which mankind first had. Nor will you ever be able to free yourself totally from the pains and wretchedness of sin. No matter how much you try, you will continue to embrace false loves and commit venial sins. Your life is like water that is drawn from a polluted well. Nevertheless, you can aim to purify your soul as much as possible. What our Lord promised to the children of Israel applies to all Christians: 'Every place where you set your foot will be yours' (Deut. 11:24). This means that you will possess all the land you desire to have. So when you come to heaven you will inherit as much of the promised land as you have longed for.

This image is to be restored by Jesus

You must seek what you have lost so that you may find it. Whoever has experienced just a fraction of the dignity the soul had through creation will hate everything in the world as if it were rotting flesh. His single desire, night and day, will be to desire, mourn, seek and pray that he may regain his dignity completely.

So far your spiritual eyes have not been fully opened. In a word I am going to tell you how you can seek, desire and find your original innocence. This word is Jesus. Of course, I do not mean the word Jesus as it is painted on a wall or written in a book or spoken by somebody's mouth or thought about in your mind. For a person who is devoid of all love may find Jesus. What I mean is Jesus Christ, that blessed person, God and man, Son of the Virgin Mary: this is whom I am talking about. He is totally good, wise and loving. He is your joy, glory, everlasting happiness, your God, your Lord and your salvation.

It is therefore good for you to have a strong desire in your heart to call Jesus' name to mind as you pray and meditate. This will push out all worldly thoughts from your mind. As you do this you will be seeking Jesus properly. As you desire Jesus or God (they are one) you will be spiritually comforted and receive love and affection and knowledge of the truth and light. At that point in time you will know nothing about any self-love or evil desires. You are completely taken up in your desire for Jesus. I do not mean Jesus as he is, but an inner experience of him. For the more you seek him the more you will find him. Take careful note of the prayer or other spiritual exercise that helps you most to find Jesus. You may find yourself asking the question: What have I lost and where can I find it? If so, you should focus your mind and heart on Jesus Christ even though you are blind and unable to see the Godhead. You should say: I long to possess Jesus whom I lost. I want him alone. I want to be where he is. I have no other joy or happiness in heaven except for him.

You may experience through your devotions or your mind some other gift from God. Whichever way you experience Jesus, never rest content with that experience. Forget what you have found and press on to know Jesus better and better, as if you do not know him yet. Even if you experience Jesus as St Paul did when he was caught up into the third heaven (2 Cor. 12:2), you will not have experienced Jesus with complete joy. No matter how much you experience of him, there is still much more for you to experience of him. So if you wish to know Jesus fully, as he is in his joy, you must never stop seeking and loving him while you live.

I would prefer to experience the Lord Jesus Christ in my heart than to experience any number of other visions or revelations or songs or smells or feelings. I believe that David meant this when he said: 'Whom have I in heaven but you? And being with you, I desire nothing on earth' (Ps. 73:25). It is as if David is saying: There is no joy in earth or heaven that can be compared with the joy of knowing you, Jesus. You must be so captivated by Jesus' love that your heart never takes satisfaction or rest in anything else. David said that he longed for God when he wrote: 'My soul is consumed with longing for your laws at all times' (Ps. 119:20). Seek Jesus in the way David did: desiring and desiring and desiring him. When you experience Jesus Christ in your prayers and meditations, hold him in your heart and do not let him go.

If you fall quickly, find him again. If you lose Jesus, seek him again. He longs to be found. He himself said: 'For everyone who asks receives; he who seeks finds; and to him who knocks, the door will be opened' (Matt. 7:8). Seeking Jesus may be painful, but finding him is a wonderful experience. If you want to find Jesus, follow the advice of the wise man: 'And if you look for it as for silver and search for it as for hidden treasure, then you will understand the fear of the Lord and find the knowledge of God' (Prov. 2:4–5). You must expel from your heart all rivals to Jesus such as your love for the world and discover true wisdom, which is Jesus.

You should be like the woman in the gospel whom Jesus spoke about: 'Or suppose a woman has ten silver coins and loses one. Does she not light a lamp, sweep the house and search carefully until she finds it?' (Luke 15:8). Who is to say that nobody would behave like this? When the woman finds the coin she calls her friends together and says to them: 'Rejoice with me; I have found my lost coin' (Luke 15:9). The coin is Jesus. You will find him if you use the light of God's word to seek him. This is what David was referring to when he said: 'Your word is a lamp to my feet and a light for my path' (Ps. 119:105). By using this light you will see where Jesus is so that you can find him. You may use a second light, the light that comes from your reason. As your Lord said: 'The eye is the lamp of the body' (Matt. 6:22). The light of your soul is reason. Through reason your soul can see all spiritual things. By using this light, so long as you do not put it under a bowl, you can discover Jesus. As Jesus said: 'Neither do people light a lamp and put it under a bowl. Instead they put it on its stand, and it gives light to everyone in the house' (Matt. 5:15). From this we deduce that your mind must be fixed on heaven and not on earthly worries. If you concentrate on this world, you are like a person grovelling around in the dust inside a house. You will attain perfection in this way. As David states: 'Who can discern his errors?' (Ps. 19:12). Nobody can be completely successful in this. You must sweep your soul clean, wash it with your tears of repentance, and then you will find your coin, Jesus. He is your inheritance.

This coin cannot be found easily. You will not find it within an hour or a day, but only after many hours, many days, and through much effort of body and soul. You must not give up the search. You must mourn deeply, and be so humble that you cry because you have lost your treasure, Jesus. Then you will discover your lost coin, Jesus. You will find him when your conscience is pure and as you experience his peaceful presence. When you do discover Jesus you should call in all your friends to rejoice with you.

Remember how merciful Jesus is. You have indeed lost Jesus. But where did you lose him? You lost him in your house, in your soul. If you had completely lost your reason as a result of the first sin, then you would never have been able to find Jesus again. But because he left you your reason he is still in your soul and has never totally left it.

However, you are never close to Jesus until you have found him. He is in you even though you have lost him. But you are not in him until you have found him. In his mercy Jesus is lost in the place where you are able to find him. You do not have to travel to Rome or Jerusalem to seek him out. All you have to do is to turn your thoughts to your own soul, where he is hidden. As the prophet has said: 'Truly you are a God who hides himself' (Isa. 45:15). He is hidden in your soul, and that is where you are to seek him. Jesus himself said in the gospels: 'The kingdom of heaven is like treasure hidden in a field. When a man found it, he hid it again, and then in his joy went and sold all he had and bought that field' (Matt. 13:44). Jesus is a treasure hidden in the soul. I am sure that when you find him in your soul, and your soul is in him, you will be happy to part with all your earthly treasures in order to possess Jesus. Jesus sleeps in your soul in the same way that he sometimes did when he was on this earth, as when he went to sleep in the boat with his disciples. When they were scared of drowning, they woke him up, and Jesus rescued them from the storm. In the same way you are to stir Jesus up through your prayers. Wake him up with your cries of desire for him. Then he will quickly wake up and help you.

I am sure that you are more often asleep to Jesus than the other way round. Often he calls to your heart with his delightful, secret voice. Your heart knows how it should discard all the clamourings of the world and listen only to Jesus' voice. As David said, in the place of our Lord: 'Listen, O daughter, consider and give ear: Forget your people and your father's house' (Ps. 45:10). That is, forget your worldly thoughts and the house of your natural desires. This is how our Lord calls you and everyone else. So what stops you from hearing and seeing him? Your worldly desires and vain thoughts make such a noise in your heart that you can neither see nor hear Jesus. So eject these noisy elements and destroy your love of sin. Welcome into your heart the love of virtues, and then you will hear your Lord speaking to you.

So long as Jesus does not find his image in you he is a stranger to you and distant from you. So aim to become like Jesus. Be humble and loving. Then Jesus will recognise you and come close to you and reveal his secrets to you. Jesus said this to his disciples: 'He who loves me will be loved by my Father, and I too will love him and show myself to him' (John 14:21). You can perform no good deed that will make you like our Lord, unless it is done in a humble and loving spirit. Jesus looks for humility and love in a person, above everything else. Jesus spoke about humility in the gospels very clearly: 'Learn from me, for I am gentle and humble in heart' (Matt. 11:29). Jesus does not say: Learn from me and go about with bare feet; or, go into the desert and fast there for forty days; or, choose disciples for yourself as I did. No. Jesus says: Learn from me and be meek. I am humble and gentle in heart. And about love Jesus said: 'A new command I give you: Love one another. As I have loved you, so you must love one another. By this all men will know that you are my disciples, if you love one another' (John 13:34–35). You are not told to perform miracles or cast out demons or preach or teach, but to love one another. If you want to be like Jesus you must be humble and loving. Now you know what love is. It is loving your neighbour as yourself.

4

DISCOVER AND DEFEAT SIN'S IMAGE

You have already heard how your soul lost its original beauty and dignity and how by God's grace this can be recovered in part in this life. Now I move on to tell you, as best I am able, how you may discover the root of sin in yourself, and how you may kill it and so recover a part of the dignity of your soul.

To do this you must stop your ordinary work. Cut off all thoughts about your human activities. You can do this easily when you are in the middle of your devotions, but it is more difficult to do when you are not performing them. With all your will and intention you must seek the grace and spiritual presence of Jesus.

This will be painful because vain thoughts will attack your heart and draw your mind after them. You will find that you have a hollow experience of Jesus and not a genuine experience of Jesus, as you would wish. Then you will discover that you have a dark image in your soul which is not God's light or love. This dark image is wrapped in layers of sin, such as pride, envy, anger, covetousness, greed and sloth. This is not the image of Jesus. It is the image of sin. St Paul refers to this as 'our old self . . . the body of sin' (Rom. 6:6). You have this black shadow cast on your soul everywhere you go. Large and small sins flow from this spring. In the same way, from the image of Jesus, once its spiritual light is in you, spring good desires and wise thoughts. From the dark image of the soul spring pride and envy which make you no better than an animal.

By now you may be wondering what this image looks like. As you do not know, I will tell you. It does not have a body. 'So what is it like?', you ask. In truth it is nothing. It is not real. You will discover this to be the case if you do as I have told you. When you stop thinking about your bodily activities you will find that your soul does not have anywhere to rest.

This nothing is none other than the darkness of conscience and an absence of God's love and light. In the same way sin is just an absence of good. If sin had shrivelled up in your soul, and if your soul had been moulded in the image of Jesus, when you concentrated on your heart you would find nothing. But you would find Jesus there. Jesus would not be there as a shadow, he would be there as a reality. He would teach you, and you would receive the light of knowledge in the place of the darkness of ignorance. You would be glad to experience the love of Jesus, and the pain of bitterness would be banished. It is because you have not let the light of Jesus flood your soul that you find that when you do withdraw from the world you only discover the emptiness and darkness of your own soul. You feel that it will be a century before you escape again and delight in your worldly pleasures and vain thoughts. It is hardly surprising that this is indeed the case. It is like a person who comes home to a house full of evil smells, smoke and a complaining wife. He will be off again in a flash. In the same way, you find no comfort in your soul. You are confronted with the black smoke of spiritual blindness or you are accused by a guilty conscience or attacked by worldly desires. You can find no peace of mind. You quickly tire of being alone, and you move out again. This is the darkness of conscience.

What you should do is work so hard that you perspire, and stay in your dark conscience. You should withdraw from the world in your mind. Then you will discover your own emptiness, blindness and darkness. This will be a painful experience. But if you want to discover Jesus you must remain for some time in the darkness of your own conscience. At this point you must take care that you bring Jesus Christ into your thoughts to fight against your own darkened mind. In your prayers and strong desires for God you must focus your attention on Jesus Christ and not on the nothingness of your own soul. Reflect on Jesus' passion and on his humility and then you will rise up in his strength. Act as if you were going to defeat this dark image. You are to hate and defeat this darkness, which is nothing, just as you do the devil. If you do not bypass this dark conscience, you will discover that Jesus is hidden within this nothingness with all his joy.

The purpose behind all this writing is to stir you, through God's grace, to seek the spiritual work I refer to. This darkness of conscience and this nothingness is the image of the first Adam. St Paul knew all about it and said: 'And just as we have borne the likeness of the earthly man, so shall we bear the likeness of the man from heaven' (1 Cor. 15:49). St Paul was weighed down so badly by this image that he cried out: 'What a wretched man I am! Who will rescue me from this body of death?' (Rom. 7:24). Then he comforted himself, and other people as well, when he said: 'Thanks be to God – through Jesus Christ our Lord!' (Rom. 7:25).

The true nature of sin and how to defeat it

I have already told you that this image is nothing. You may not understand this, since nothing can be nothing other than nothing. I will now go on to explain more simply what I think this image means.

This image is a false inordinate love of yourself. Seven

sins flow from this source: pride, envy, anger, sloth, covetousness, greed and debauchery. Here is something that you are able to understand. If one of these sins is a deadly sin it can rob you of your state of Christian love, and if it is a venial sin it can remove your desire for Christian love. You may now feel that this image is more than nothing. It is bad because it originates in your self-love with the seven sins, as I have said.

But, you may ask, how can this be true? Have I not forsaken the world and become enclosed in a monastery? I do not have any dealings with people, I do not tell people off, I do not buy or sell, and I have no business affairs to attend to in the world. By God's mercy I am pure and I do not indulge in worldly pleasures. In addition to this, I pray, watch and engage in spiritual and bodily exercises as much as I can. So how can this image exist in me to the extent that you say?

Even if you do all the deeds you mention, and more besides, what I say remains true. You spend your time trying to dam the seven rivers while you ignore the source they flow from. You are like a person who had a polluted well which supplied water to other wells. He stopped the polluted water flowing from his well to the other wells, but he did nothing about the polluted spring and thought that he had solved the problem. But he found that the water from the spring seeped through the soil and so ruined his whole garden, even though he could not see any water flowing. It is the same with you if you have succeeded by God's grace in stopping the flow of the seven rivers. Everything will seem fine, but you must beware of the spring within you. If you are not able to cure that, you will find that all the flowers in the garden of your soul are polluted, no matter how beautiful they may appear to be.

You may now want to know how to go about curing the polluted spring. I will now tell you how to recognise this image if it is in you. Then you will know how to stop it. Because pride is the principal sin, I will start with it.

5

THE FIRST OF THE DEADLY SINS, PRIDE

Pride is nothing other than loving yourself and thinking that you are excellent. The more you love and esteem yourself, the prouder you are. When you think that you are holier, wiser, better and more virtuous than others, then you will know that this black image is stirring in your heart. If you think that God has given you grace to serve him better than others, and if you revel in this view of yourself, you are indeed being vain. You may succeed in hiding this from other people, but it is quite clear to God.

You may feel that you cannot help being proud because these feelings often overtake you against your will and so you do not feel that they are sinful at all. Or, if they are sinful thoughts, then they are only venial.

The answer to this is that all such rising of pride, as with any other sin which flows from the corruption of this evil image, is not sinful just because you experience it. It only becomes sinful when you cherish and hang on to such thoughts in your heart. It is then a venial sin or a deadly sin, depending on how much you love and welcome these desires.

All Christians who have been baptised in water and by the Holy Spirit receive God's grace because of Christ's passion. But it is a deadly sin for a Jew or Muslim to become proud because they do not believe in Jesus Christ. For St Paul teaches that whatever is done without faith in Christ is sin. But Christians are privileged, through God's mercy, so that when they experience these proud feelings they are not sinning but enduring the pain of original sin.

It is not always easy to distinguish between venial and deadly sins in this case, but I will now give you my opinion on this. When the heart delights in and welcomes these stirrings of pride with open arms, then this pride is deadly sin. This is a deadly sin because pride was not opposed and because a deliberate decision was taken to allow pride to become a god.

You may think that nobody would ever choose pride as his god. My answer to this is that I am not able to specify in every instance when somebody commits a deadly sin in connection with pride. However, I can tell you that as a general principle there are two kinds of pride, one is bodily and the other is spiritual. Bodily pride belongs to worldly men and spiritual pride is the preserve of hypocrites and heretics. St Paul speaks of worldly men living in this kind of pride: 'For if you live according to the sinful nature, you will die' (Rom. 8:13). People who take pride in their own evil selves live in deadly sin.

You may ask who would choose to love and esteem himself in preference to God? My answer is that anyone who thinks himself better than others and parades himself around assuming this to be true sins in this way. These people behave like this even if it means breaking God's commandments and not being loving towards their neighbours. However, the person who sins in this way will protest that he does not choose pride as his god. He deceives himself because his actions prove that he has indeed chosen pride as his god.

People who are self-centred but who do not break God's commands, and who do not stop loving their neighbours as a result, sin in a venial but not a deadly way.

Contemplatives who have given up their lives to the

service of God may still find that pride rears up in their hearts. Such people may enjoy these proud thoughts to start with because they are not recognised for what they are. But this is only a venial sin, because contemplatives will then reprove themselves and set their wills to fight pride and ask for God's help and mercy to do this. Our Lord, in his mercy, will forgive him for welcoming pride in the first place. The contemplative will be rewarded in this way for fighting against pride.

Our Lord is gracious enough to bestow this favour on all who belong to a religious order which is approved of by the holy church. This is extended to anyone who serves God in a spiritual way and who turns his back on the ways of the world.

God's special servants in his holy church are those who forsake the pleasures of this world and delight themselves in their prayers and other godly devotions. Such people may be priests or laymen, anybody who is concerned for the salvation of his soul and the love of God. As they pursue this goal God will give them more and more of his grace and his love throughout their lives. In heaven these people will receive greater rewards than those people who have not offered themselves up wholly to God's service, either openly or secretly. All such people I call God's servants. These servants do not sin in a venial way when they momentarily welcome the stirrings of pride in their hearts. The settled disposition of their hearts is to please God. So when they are overtaken by pride or by any other sin because of the weakness of human nature, they do not commit deadly sins.

I am telling you this for your comfort, and also for the comfort of all who live in enclosed religious orders. Through God's mercy they will receive a special reward and special worship in heaven. They have privileges which other souls do not possess, no matter how holy they become. They never desire to exchange their position for any role in the world. They do not want to lose their special heavenly reward.

To make sure that I am not misunderstood in this I will state it very clearly. Our Lord gives two rewards in heaven to the souls he chooses. The first reward is the sovereign and principal one, called the essential reward. This is knowing and loving God in heaven in proportion to the God-given love the soul received on earth. This is the best of the two rewards, and is sovereign because it is God himself. It is the possession of all people who are saved, regardless of their position in the church. Their reward is linked to how much they have loved God during their lives. The person who loves God most on earth will be the person who receives most of God's love in heaven. This is the sovereign, or essential reward. This reward is open to everyone to receive: to men and women, to lords and ladies, to knights and squires, to merchants and farm labourers. Such people may receive more of this reward than some priests or friars or monks or canons or members of an enclosed religious order. Why is this? Because they have loved God so much.

The other reward is secondary and not essential for everyone to receive. It is a reward bestowed by our Lord on people who voluntarily engage in special deeds beyond their duty. Doctors of the holy church place three types of people in this category: martyrs, preachers and celibates. These deeds exceed all others, and the reward they receive is called an aureole. It is beyond the sovereign or essential reward of God's love which is also given to those who receive the aureole reward as well as to other people. If other deeds are sincerely performed, such as belonging to an enclosed order, they will be specially commended by the holy church.

After belonging to an enclosed order come the priests who either care for people's souls or administer the sacraments. Then there are those people who, on account of the sacrifice of our Lord Jesus Christ, are particularly devoted to God, seek to please God and be helpful to their neighbour. These special deeds are commended by the church and by our Lord. When they are performed for God's glory they will enable such people to receive the appropriate reward in heaven. Bishops and rulers in the church are above these deeds as far as the second reward is concerned. This is confirmed by the prophet Daniel: 'As for you, go your way till the end. You will rest, and then at the end of the days you will rise to receive your allotted inheritance' (Dan. 12:13). When the angel had shown Daniel God's secrets, he said to him: 'Go and rest now as you die and you will receive a prophet's reward on the last day.' It is quite true that on judgement day Daniel will receive the second reward, the reward beyond the sovereign reward. Members of enclosed religious orders, together with those who have performed exceptional deeds and have devoted themselves to worshipping God, will receive the same reward as Daniel, which is beyond what other men will receive on the judgement day.

Why pride in heretics and hypocrites is a deadly sin

Heretics commit a deadly sin when they indulge in pride because they indulge themselves in their own thinking which they believe is true. If these thoughts are opposed to the teaching of the holy church, the heretic sticks to his own opinion and so acts as if he is God himself. He deceives himself here. For the teaching of the church and the teaching of God are so united that if anybody opposes one of them he is at the same time opposing the other as well. So the person who claims to follow God and yet opposes the teachings of the church which have been made by its head, who is over all other Christians, is a liar. He is not choosing God, rather he is in opposition to God and loving himself. This is a deadly sin. When he thinks that he is pleasing God most he is displeasing God most. He is blind and unable to see what he is doing.

The wise writer of the book of Proverbs refers to this blindness and to the heretic's mistaken trust in himself when he writes: 'There is a way that seems right to a man, but in the end it leads to death' (Prov. 14:12). This is the essence of heresy. Other deadly sins prick their consciences, but heretics believe that they are right. They think that nobody teaches so accurately as they do, and their consciences give them no warning signals and their hearts are devoid of humility. Unless God gives him the grace of humility the heretic will end up in hell. The heretic, however, will carry on believing that he has done well and that he will receive heavenly rewards on account of all his teaching.

The hypocrite also commits deadly sins of pride. A person who revels and delights in himself is a hypocrite.

A person may perform many good physical and spiritual deeds. Then the enemy sows the thought in his mind that he should think how good he is, how holy he is and how well thought of he is in the eyes of men and in the eyes of God. The hypocrite believes that this is all true because he feels that his good deeds exceed those of everybody else. When his mind convinces him about the truth of this, his heart is filled with great love and delight in himself. He believes that he is so full of grace that he is captivated by such reasoning and puts all other thoughts out of his mind. He revels in this spiritual pride and takes great delight in it. He clings on to it and feeds it all the time. In this frame of mind he carries out all his prayers, devotions, wearing of sackcloth and other duties. He even allows a tear to drop from his eyes and he believes that he is completely safe. He is utterly mistaken. Everything he does he does to please himself, and nothing is done out of love for God. This is the root of his sin. It is not that he deliberately chose to sin, but that this revelling in what he takes to be good is sinful in itself. It is sinful because he does not try to resist it in any way. He thinks that he is rejoicing in God when he is not, and that is a deadly sin. Job said of the hypocrite: 'The joy of the godless lasts but a moment. Though his pride reaches to the heavens and his head touches the clouds, he will perish for ever, like his own dung' (Job 20:5–7). A hypocrite may indulge in self-love and good deeds all his life, and receive praises from everybody else for his good deeds. But at the end of his life this will prove to be nothing other than sadness and pain.

You may object to this and say that you find it hard to believe that people who confuse God's joy and their own joy exist.

I am not going to answer this question, although I could. I will just tell you one thing. There are many hypocrites. They do not believe that they are hypocrites, but they are. Others fear that they may be hypocrites, but they are not. Only God knows who the hypocrites are. Whoever lives in humble reverence before God will not be deceived, and whoever thinks that he is safe may quickly fall. For St Paul says: 'If anyone thinks he is something when he is nothing, he deceives himself' (Gal. 6:3).

Be humble and loving; how you can know how proud you are

From what I have said you may derive comfort in the way you live and also with regard to humility. It may well be true that in heaven you will receive God's special reward. Nevertheless, it should shame you that many wives, many women who live in the world, are closer to God and love him more than you, even though you belong to a closed religious order. But if you strive to be as loving as they are then you will receive a greater reward from God than the sovereign or essential reward, which is what they receive. Because you belong to a closed religious order you will have the second reward, while other people will not. If you want to do well, you will be humble and forget your privileges and think of yourself as nothing. This is the truth: you are nothing in yourself. Your work is to destroy sin and to pursue love and humility and such virtues that are derived from them.

For a long time I have forgotten the image I spoke about, to which I now return. This is how you may know how much pride you have. View yourself carefully and do not flatter yourself. You are proud if you love the praise of other people. You are proud if you believe that other people ought to praise you. You are proud if you think that you should be praised for your addresses more than other people are praised. You are also proud when you are hurt by criticisms of foolish and hypocritical people. You are proud if you are not prepared to suffer undeserved abuse. You may appear ever so holy in the sight of men, yet this is but a sign of the dark image of pride in you. In themselves these sins may appear to be venial and of little consequence, but they point to deep-seated pride in your heart. Your nature is so polluted by pride that it is difficult to do any good deed that remains untainted by pride. All such deeds are obnoxious in our Lord's sight. I am not saying that these good deeds are useless. But I am saying that they are not as good as they would be if they were rooted in humility. Then you would have a pure heart and receive God's love. You must not allow your heart to indulge in your own vanity, allowing full rein to your pride. You must guard your heart against feeling pride. The only way you will succeed in this is by being diligent, as I shall tell you later on.

6

ENVY AND ANGER AND THEIR BRANCHES

If you turn to the roots of the image of pride you will find envy and anger there. Envy and anger produce many branches which fight against the love you should have for your neighbour. Here is a list of the branches which envy and anger produce: hatred, evil suspicion, unwise judgements, melancholy, despising other people, unkindness, backbiting and other ways of speaking badly about people, disliking people, blaming other people wrongly, misconstruing other people's words and deeds, ill will towards those who speak against you, delight in the pain of others, bitterness towards sinful people and others who do not think in the same way as you do, a strong desire, under the guise of love and justice, that sinful people will be punished for their sin.

At first, these feelings may appear to be good. But when you examine them closely you will find that they are worldly and unspiritual and are more against the person than against his sin. You should love the man, no matter how sinful he is. You should hate sin in every man, no matter who he may be. Many are deceived about this and embrace the bitter for the sweet and the darkness for the light. They are not taking any notice of the prophet Isaiah when he said: 'Woe to those who call evil good and good evil, who put darkness for light and light for darkness' (Isa. 5:20). People do this when they hate the person rather than his sin, while they pretend all the time to be hating the sin. It is a special skill to make the correct distinction.

It is an art to love people and still to hate their sin

You do yourself no credit if you watch and fast until you give yourself a headache. You will derive no benefit from running barefoot to Rome or Jerusalem. You will not gain anything if you make people hang on your every word as you preach. You will not achieve anything by building churches or chapels, or by feeding the poor or by building hospitals. But you will have achieved something worthwhile if you truly love your neighbour and hate his sin. It is true that all the above-mentioned deeds are good, but they are performed by good and bad people alike. Anybody could do them if he has the inclination and the means. I do not think you achieve much by doing what everybody else can do. But to love your neighbour and hate his sin is something that only good men can do. And they can only do it if they have received God's grace for this. They are unable to achieve this through their own efforts. As St Paul has said: 'God has poured out his love into our hearts by the Holy Spirit, whom he has given us' (Rom. 5:5). This is much more difficult to achieve. Without this gift, no matter what good deeds are performed, nobody will be able to reach heaven. Through this gift all the deeds of a good man are indeed good. All of God's other gifts are given to both the elect and to the reprobate, and to the good and to the bad. This gift of love is reserved for some specially selected souls.

It is important that you learn this difficult lesson. A good man will fast, watch, go on a pilgrimage, genuinely forsake all the pleasures of the world and so receive his heavenly reward out of his deep love for God. A hypocrite will perform the same deeds, but out of his love for himself, and he receives his reward here and now. A faithful preacher of God's word who is filled with love and humility and who has been sent by God and commissioned by the church will receive God's special reward, the aureole. On the other hand, a hypocrite or a heretic who have no humility or love and who have not been sent either by God or the church, receive their reward now. A good man who lives his life out of love for God in the world may build many churches, chapels, abbeys and hospitals, and do many other merciful good deeds. He will receive his blissful heavenly reward not because of the deeds in themselves, but on account of the God-given love in which he did the good deeds. Another person could do exactly the same good deeds but in a spirit of vanity, looking to the world for applause. He has his reward now. The reason for all this is that one person has love and the other person does not. Only our Lord is able to tell which person acts from love.

We learn two lessons from this. First, in our hearts we should love all men and think well about all their deeds which appear to be good, even if the people who perform them are bad in God's sight. The only exceptions to this are heretics and those who have been excommunicated. We should never be in their company. We should never accept their good deeds so long as they stay in a state of rebellion against God and the holy church. If a worldly or excommunicated person builds a church or feeds the poor, you will know for certain that his deeds amount to nothing and they should be treated as such. Even if a heretic who is in open rebellion against the holy church should make one hundred thousand converts through his preaching, he will not benefit at all from this action. These people are clearly not loving God. No man can achieve anything if he does not love God.

Second, it is hard to understand how to love your neighbour properly. This is clearly seen in the following words of St Paul: 'If I speak in the tongues of men and of angels, but have not love, I am only a resounding gong or a clanging cymbal. If I have the gift of prophecy and can fathom all mysteries and all knowledge, and if I have a faith that can move mountains, but have not love, I am nothing. If I give all I possess to the poor and surrender my body to the flames, but have not love, I gain nothing' (1 Cor. 13:1–3). St Paul is teaching here that a person may perform every kind of good deed and have no love in his heart. This love is nothing other than loving God and loving his neighbour as himself. How can such a wretched person take any pleasure in anything he does, since everything he does is devoid of love for his neighbour? This kind of love cannot be achieved by his own efforts, since it is a free gift from God which is only given to humble souls, as St Paul says. Who then will dare to be so bold and declare: I have Christ, or, I am doing a loving act? Only a humble man can say this and know that it is true. Other people just hope that they have this love. But the humble person experiences it for himself and knows that he possesses it. St Paul was humble, and so he could say: 'Who shall separate us from the love of Christ? Shall trouble or hardship or persecution or famine or nakedness or danger or sword?' His reply to his question is: 'No, in all these things we are more than conquerors through him who loved us. For I am convinced that neither death nor life, neither angels nor demons, neither the present nor the future, nor any powers, neither height nor depth, nor anything else in all creation, will be able to separate us from the love of God that is in Christ Jesus our Lord' (Rom. 8:35, 37–39). Many people perform charitable acts who are devoid of love, as I have said. To reprove a sinner for his sin so that he can turn from it is an act of love. But to hate the sinner and not the sin is not a loving act. Only the person who is genuinely humble is able to distinguish the sinner from the sin. Even someone who has studied all the teachings of the moral philosophers is not able to make the correct judgement here. With all his philosophy he would be able to hate the sin he sees in others, for he hates sin in himself, but he would not be able to love the sinner. Even the most learned person who has read all the theological books, if he is not genuinely humble, will stumble at this point and mistake the one for the other. Humility enables a man to receive a gift from God which it is impossible to gain through any human effort. So the humble man can hate sin and at the same time love the sinner.

You may now begin to be upset by all I have said, as love cannot be acquired from anything that you do. What should you do, then?

My answer to this is that there is nothing so difficult to achieve as love. This is true in relation to trying to gain it through our own efforts and work. On the other hand, there is no gift that is so easy to receive as love. This is because love is God's gift which he freely bestows on us. You wonder how you may receive this gift? If you are meek and gentle in spirit, you will receive it. You can do nothing more than to be humble. You must not be afraid, because nothing can be achieved so easily as love. Be humble, and you will receive love. As St James says: 'God opposes the proud but gives grace to the humble' (Jas. 4:6). This grace is love. You will have love in proportion to your humility. If you are only humble in your will and not in your emotions, you have imperfect love. This is sufficient for salvation, as David says: 'Thine eyes did see my substance, yet being unperfect' (Ps. 139:16, AV). If you have complete humility you will have complete love, which is best. The lesser kind of love is necessary for salvation, and we should always be seeking it. If you were to ask me who is completely humble, my only reply is: A person is humble who truly knows himself as he is.

How to know how much anger and envy are hidden in your heart

We return again in our thinking to this image of pride. Try to imagine how much anger and envy is hidden in your heart which you are unaware of. When anger and envy against your neighbour rise in your heart, examine yourself carefully. The more you find that this anger and envy rises in your heart, the greater is the image of pride in you. The more you complain impatiently against God about trials or sickness sent by God, or about injuries suffered at the hand of your neighbour, the less the image of Jesus has been formed in you. I am not saying that this kind of grumbling and worldly anger are deadly sins. They do, however, prevent you from having a pure heart and a clear conscience, without which you cannot have complete love and live the contemplative life. This is the purpose behind everything that I am saying. You should not only purify your heart of deadly sins, but also, as much as is possible, from venial sins. Then the root cause for your sin will be pulled out by the grace of Jesus Christ.

Even if for a time you experience no bad thoughts against your neighbour, do not think that all your anger has disappeared. You have not yet become lord and master of the virtue of love. All your neighbour has to do is upset you with an unkind word and then we will see if your heart is perfectly loving. The more you are upset and think badly of your neighbour, the further you are from love.

Here is the way to love your neighbour perfectly. Do not be upset by the way he walks or by any of his bodily movements. Do not secretly hate him in your heart. Do not despise him, or judge him, or undervalue him, or think of him as being nothing. The more he acts badly towards you, the more compassion you must show him, as if he were a madman. Believe that it is impossible for you to hate him because it is the nature of love to be good. Pray for your neighbour, help him, long for him to change his life. Do this with all your heart and not just with the outward show of a hypocrite. If you do these things, you will be showing perfect love towards your neighbour.

St Stephen displayed this perfect love when he prayed for the people who were stoning him to death. Christ taught about this love when he told his disciples that they should be perfect: 'Love your enemies and pray for those who persecute you' (Matt. 5:44). If you aspire to be one of Christ's disciples, you must be like him in this respect. Learn to love your enemies and sinful people, as these too are your neighbours. Consider how Christ loved his deadly enemy Judas. Think about how good and gentle Christ was to Judas, even though Christ knew that he was damned. Christ still chose him to be one of his apostles and sent him out to preach with the rest of the apostles. Christ gave him the power to perform miracles. Christ encouraged him in word and deed in the same way that he encouraged the other apostles. Christ washed Judas' feet and fed him with his precious blood and preached to him along with the other apostles. Christ spoke to Judas quietly so the other apostles would not hear. Christ did not call him names, or despise him or speak badly of him. If Christ had done all these things, he would have only been saying the truth. In addition to this, when Judas kissed Christ, Christ called him his friend. Christ showed all this love to Judas, whom he knew was damned. Christ genuinely loved Judas and never pretended to love him. Judas never deserved to have any gift from God or any token of love as he was so wicked. Nevertheless, it was right that our Lord should show Judas how good and loving he was to everyone, including Judas.

I am not saying that Christ loved Judas because of his sin, or that he loved him because he had chosen him, as Christ loved St Peter. But Christ did love Judas because he was his creator, and he showed him tokens of his love so that Judas could have been changed. You must follow Christ's example in this as much as possible. Even though you belong to a closed religious order, you still have a heart with which you can love your neighbour in the way I have told you.

Some people may think that they love Christ fully and follow Christ's teaching perfectly. Some people, for example, who preach and teach and have few earthly possessions like Christ, believe that they are like this. But if these people are unable to be like Christ in the love he showed towards his neighbours, then they are fooling themselves. If you cannot show unconditional love for your neighbour, no matter how well or badly he behaves towards you, then you only deceive yourself when you think that you have Christian love in your heart. The closer you imagine that you approximate to Christ in this, the further you are from him in reality. Christ told his would-be disciples: 'A new command I give you: Love one another. As I have loved you, so you must love one another. All men will know that you are my disciples, if you love one another' (John 13:34–35).

You may wonder how you are genuinely to love the bad person in the same way that you love the good person.

Here is my reply to your question. You must love good people and bad people, but not for the same reason. You know that you are commanded to love your neighbour as yourself. You must love yourself in God, or else for God's sake. You love yourself in God when you are virtuous and righteous through God's grace. But you do not love yourself and are only loving God when you are only being virtuous and righteous for the sake of it. You love yourself for God's sake when you desire to escape from your deadly sins and become righteous and virtuous. Then you are not loving yourself as you are, as you are not righteous, but you are loving yourself for what you will become.

You should love your neighbour in the same way. If he is good and righteous, you should love him only in God, because he can only be good and righteous through God's gifts. In this way you can love God, who is goodness and righteousness, in this person. Then you will be loving this person more than if he were either bad or had fallen into deadly sin. This is the way you are to love your enemies and those you know who are not living in God's grace. But you do not love them on account of any goodness or righteousness in them, for they are bad and unrighteous, but you love them for God, in the hope that they may become good and righteous. The only thing you are to hate in them is sin and all that is contrary to righteousness. This is how I understand St Augustine's teaching. Make a distinction between loving the person and hating his sin, as you love your neighbour. Only the person who is genuinely humble, or seeks to be so, can love his neighbour in this way.

7

COVETOUSNESS

Dig up again the image of pride in your heart and thoroughly examine it. Then you will discover that covetousness and the love of earthly things makes up a large proportion of the image, though at first sight this does not appear to be the case. You may be confined to your cell and you may have forsaken riches and having much in the world, but have you really forsaken your desire for these things? I fear that this is not the case, because it is easier to give up worldly things than to give up your longing for them. Perhaps you have not eradicated covetousness, but have rather changed from coveting big things to coveting small things. You no longer covet pounds, just pence; you no longer covet silver plates, just cheap plates. This is only a superficial change. You are not a trader. The examples may be childish, but they illustrate truth. If you do not believe what I am teaching, give yourself this test. Here are evidences that covetousness exists in the image. If you love and take delight in anything, no matter how tiny and insignificant it may be in itself, in such a way that your heart is moved with a desire for it, you are being covetous. If you long for anything that you do not possess so that your rest in God is upset, you may be sure that you are being covetous. Here is another test for you. Are you ever troubled if anything you have is borrowed or taken away from you? If so, you are covetous. If you find yourself angry against the person who has deprived you of your possessions, you may be sure that you are in love with worldly things. This is how men of the world react when they have things taken away from them. They are dispirited and angry and contend with the person who has deprived them of their possessions. You do all this in the privacy of your heart. But God observes this. You are worse than the worldly man. You are supposed to have renounced worldly possessions, whereas the man of the world has not done this, so he is excused for trying lawfully to restore his possessions.

You may say that you have to possess certain essential things which are common to you and to worldly people. I agree with you. But you should not love these things for their own sake, you should not cling to them, and you should not feel upset if they are taken away from you. As St Gregory says, you can tell how much you love something by the degree of sorrow you experience when you lose it. If you truly desired spiritual things, your heart would have been healed of its craving for earthly things. Once you have but a glimpse of spiritual things, your desire for worldly possessions will vanish into thin air.

It is wrong to long to possess anything other than essentials. It is also not right to focus your attention on something that you do not have but desire. But it is not wrong to make use of possessions, so long as you do not set your heart on them.

It is at this point that I fear that many people who have taken vows of poverty are hampered in their pursuit of God. I am not accusing any particular person or attacking any one way of life. Each way of living has things which are commendable as well as things one can criticise. I am now speaking to anybody who has taken a vow of poverty. This vow may have been a religious one or a secular one. You will never have clear spiritual sight so long as you cherish the love of earthly things in your heart. As St Augustine said to our Lord: 'Lord, a man loves you little so long as he loves anything as well as you.' The more you love any earthly thing, the less of God's love there is in your heart. Love of earthly things does not make you totally unloving. But love of earthly things stifles your love of God and your love of your neighbour. It prevents you from being openly charitable and stops you receiving that special reward in heaven for being completely poor in spirit. If you could see the reward, you would realise how much of a loss it is. If you appreciated how great this heavenly reward is, you would gladly give up all love of earthly things, since the reward lasts for ever. You would not become immersed in anything that would prevent you from receiving this reward. But God knows I am speaking about more than I have myself experienced.

However, I do pray that, by God's grace, you will do what I say, even though it is beyond my personal experience. I will be greatly encouraged to see somebody else receive more of God's grace than I have.

Now you will appreciate how much covetousness strangles your spiritual love of God. You can see how much more tightly it squeezes out God's love from worldly people who do nothing else than make themselves rich. They take pleasure only in worldly things because this is the only type of life they know. I will not say any more about them, because I am not writing to them. What I am telling you is that if they want to see, or if they could see what they are doing, they would change their lives.

8

EATING AND DRINKING AND GLUTTONY

There is yet more to observe in this dark image. I am referring to love of yourself in gluttony, laziness and lust. These sins make a man appear to be like an animal and distance him from his inner love of God and dim his sight of spiritual things. You may raise the objection that it is necessary to eat, drink and sleep, and so you are not sinning when you do these things.

My answer to this is that it is indeed possible to eat, drink and sleep without committing any sin. But you must only engage in these necessities of life to the extent that nature requires. You must not take any pleasure in them beyond this. You must only engage in them for your spiritual benefit, and not for your own bodily pleasure.

I have not actually managed to achieve this myself, and I do not know how to improve. I know how to eat in a natural way, but I do not know how to eat in a better way unless God gives me the grace to do so. St Paul had learned how to be content through the grace of God. He said: 'I have learned to be content whatever the circumstances. I know what it is to be in need, and I know what it is to have plenty. I have learned the secret of being content in any and every situation, whether well fed or hungry, whether living in plenty or in want. I can do everything through him who gives me strength' (Phil. 4:11–13). St Augustine says to our Lord: 'Lord you have taught me that I should think of food as a medicine. Hunger is a disease and food is a medicine for it.' So it is not sinful to eat so long as you are only eating for necessity's sake. But eating becomes sinful when you take delight in overeating.

It is hard to distinguish between eating for necessity's sake and indulging in overeating. It is hard to accept the one without crossing over the boundary into the other.

The principle in this is that where we eat for necessity's sake it is not sinful. No matter how holy a person may be, he still needs to eat, drink and sleep. So when you do overeat, because you eat for necessity's sake your sin is not very great. It is quite a different matter for the person who lives to delight in eating and just indulges himself in food all the time. When a person does this he is committing deadly sins. He is loving himself more than God. A person who wallows in a deadly sin like pride is so blinded by the devil that he feels that he has no power to resist the sin. He collapses as soon as he is attacked by the sin and becomes like a carcass for vultures. Because he is in the habit of giving in to deadly sins he is easy prey for the sin of greed to take him over. In contrast to this other people strive to please God, through God's grace, in everything they do, whether it be eating or drinking or doing good deeds. When this person lapses into greed and overeats and takes great pleasure in eating he is saved from committing a deadly sin because the grace of our Lord Jesus is with him. He continues to love God and to do good works, and he confesses his temporary falling into greed and he manages to withstand greed when next tempted. If this happens, our Lord is merciful and forgives his venial sins concerning eating and drinking because he is humble at heart.

When you fall into this kind of greed you are not committing a very serious sin. The cause of this sin is easy to discover. It comes from the necessity to eat and drink. You should not treat yourself too severely if you fall into this type of greed. However, you must be vigilant against all other sins, whether they are venial or deadly. You must know where the sins spring from and take every possible precaution against leaving yourself open to attacks from them. You cannot apply this principle to eating and drinking because you need to eat and drink to stay alive. But you can eat and drink without indulging your bodily desires in overeating and drunkenness. It is, however, possible to live without gluttony, and this is indeed how you should live. You should set yourself against all gluttonous deeds and all thoughts of gluttony, and you should also fight against the sinful root of gluttony as it rises up in your heart.

You should engage in this battle against the root of gluttony with the spiritual weapon of prayer, and not just with bodily penances. Remember that no matter how much you fast, pray and scourge yourself you will never become pure and chaste unless God gives you the gift of humility.

It is easier to kill your body than to mortify your body against lust and gluttony. But a humble soul, through the grace of Jesus, will uproot this sin of gluttony and so become genuinely chaste in body and soul.

This is exactly the same in the case of pride and covetousness, as well as with other sins. You may live as if you were not proud or covetous, and you may be purified from the root of these sins. But it is different with greed. Greed is so linked with our need to satisfy our human appetite that the temptation to fall into greed will be with us all our lives. So you must always be alert to fight against the excesses of eating and drinking which will be around trying to catch you out unawares. They will pretend to be just and reasonable bodily appetites. You must attack these evil onslaughts and hold your ground.

Be constantly on the alert against sin, especially spiritual sins

You are half blind if you spend more time opposing the sins of overeating and overdrinking and ignore the battle against the sins of pride, covetousness, lust and envy. These latter sins are less well understood because they are more spiritual and less easy to detect. I call you half blind because you fail to see your spiritual sins and how repulsive they are in God's sight. If a person could view his spiritual sins in the same way that God does, he would loathe his own evil or his own anger against his neighbour much more than any feelings of greed or lust. But this is not the case with most people. They are more worried about a physical sin than a spiritual sin such as vanity. Such people are not wise. They would change their minds if they studied the scriptures and the writings of the great teachers in the church. But I will not go into this now.

I am not saying that people who commit greed or lust have not sinned. The seriousness of their sin depends on how much they desired to sin and whether they were led into it through other circumstances. I want you to understand the seriousness of different kinds of sin. Spiritual sins are more serious sins than bodily sins. I advise you to run away from both kinds of sin. You must understand that bodily sins like desiring food and drink and other desires of the body which exceed your necessities are not serious sins so long as you are generally loving God in your heart. However, for the soul who is seeking a pure heart and longing for a closer spiritual walk with God, these sins of greed and lust will weigh heavily and should be cut out. For the spirit cannot be at rest within the soul so long as the body has not lost its appetite for outward things.

If you want to have a pure heart you must fight against the longings of your body, but you do not have to oppose the source from which these longings spring. For they stem from your needs, such as natural hunger which you have to experience and must respond to in the correct way. Think of eating as taking medicine. Take the appropriate amount to make your body well again. Then you will be in a position to serve God with your body and soul.

You know full well that if you are preoccupied with thinking about great pain or too much fasting then your spiritual devotions will be adversely affected. Unless you are very advanced in the contemplative life you will not make spiritual progress when your thoughts are dominated by physical distractions. It is true that physical pain can increase your desire to love God in your devotions and that it does not always have to diminish it. However, I believe that physical trials are more beneficial to your spiritual life if they come when you contemplate because you are then more aware of spiritual longings than any physical longings.

How to correct wrong eating and drinking

You should look after your body carefully, according to what is a reasonable necessity. Then leave it in God's hands to send you either good health or sickness. Receive whatever God gives gratefully and not grudgingly.

Follow the advice I am giving. Within reason, you are to eat the food you are given, accepting happily, knowing that you need it. You must also be alert to the temptations that come from this. You can be tempted to eat too much as well as too little. If you believe that you have eaten too much, you may find that your heart is filled with remorse and that your conscience makes you aware that you have indulged yourself. When this happens you may become sad, downcast and fed up with yourself. Then you must turn your heart to your good Lord Jesus, admit your wretchedness and ask him to forgive you. Tell him that you resolve to change your life, and pray to him for his forgiveness. Then do not think about the matter any more. Do not fight against the vice as if you wanted to kill it, because it is not worthy of such great attention. And in any case you will not be able to effect such a change. Turn to some other spiritual or physical activity so that you may benefit from other virtues such as humility and love. You will make much more progress in every aspect of your spiritual life if you give yourself to being humble and loving. You will then discover that other virtues such as chastity and abstinence are changed for the better. If you concentrate on the two virtues of love and humility, you will make more progress in a single year than if you scourged yourself all night and day for seven years trying to deal with greed and lust.

You will be fully occupied if you pursue humility and love diligently. If you become humble and loving you will know how you should eat and drink and provide for all your other bodily necessities. Nobody need know how you have decided to behave in these matters unless you choose to tell them. You will no longer be plagued with a bad conscience and be full of worries about your longings and desires. You will live peacefully with a clear conscience. I have spoken at greater length about this matter than I intended, but I nevertheless trust that God will make everything clear to you.

From what I have said you will see to a certain extent this sinful image and understand how it opposes you in your spiritual life. The gospel relates how Abraham spoke to the rich man who was in hell in this way: 'Between us and you a great chasm has been fixed' (Luke 16:26). There is thick darkness between us and you so that we cannot come to you and you cannot come to us. Similarly, the dark image in my soul and in your soul may be likened to a chaos or great darkness. It prevents us from approaching Abraham, who is Jesus, and it stops him from coming to us.

9

THE FIVE WINDOWS OF THE DARK IMAGE

Lift up a lantern and you will see that there are five windows in this dark image through which sins enter. As the prophet says: 'Death has climbed in through our windows' (Jer. 9:21). The five windows are the five senses. Through these five senses the soul indulges itself in earthly things which are opposed to its own spiritual nature. The soul is intrigued to know about unusual things, and the other senses have a similar tendency. When an immature soul gives in to these senses he hinders his own spiritual life. So you must close these windows and only open them when it is necessary to do so.

You would find this easy to do if you had a clear view of how wonderful your own soul was originally and how it still would be if it was not clothed in the blackness of this horrible image. You do not have such understanding, and so you behave like a brute beast and seek to satisfy yourself away from your soul. Our Lord speaks about this sternly in the Bible: 'Tell me, you whom I love, where you graze your flock and where you rest your sheep at midday' (Song of Sol. 1:7). Here we are taught that the soul is made in the image of God and is good in its nature. It was weak in the body of a woman, and because of the first sin you do not know yourself or take delight in the food of angels. Therefore you turn outwards and seek your pleasures in bodily delights and behave like a wild animal. You allow your thoughts and emotions to feed on these evil desires. You should be ashamed of yourself.

So turn away from pig's food and turn back to your inner self. Behave like a beggar and ask your Lord Jesus to make you rich and he will happily give you what you seek because he is rich. Stop behaving like a wild animal that only has delight in its bodily senses. When you do this the Lord Jesus will give you everything that you need. He will take you into his wine cellar to drink from a magnificent selection of wines. A chosen soul, rejoicing in our Lord, said of him in the Bible: 'He has taken me to the banquet hall' (Song of Sol. 2:4). You have forsaken indulging in bodily pleasures which only bring pain, and the Lord Jesus has rewarded you for this. First, the Lord Jesus has allowed you to enter his banqueting room and to know him for yourself. Then he has taken you into his cellar to taste the wine of heavenly joy. These are no mere words of a wretched man who lives in sin. They are the words of the bride of our Lord found in the Bible. I am telling you this so that you can draw in your soul from outside and follow the Lord Jesus more closely.

Your desire to know more about this has drawn more from my heart than I had originally planned to tell you. I will now show you when bodily sins are venial and when they are deadly. Our Lord says this in the gospel: 'A certain man was preparing a great banquet and invited many guests. At the time of the banquet he sent his servant to tell those who had been invited, "Come, for everything is now ready." But they all alike began to make excuses. The first said, "I have just bought a field, and I must go and see it. Please excuse me." Another said, "I have just bought five yoke of oxen, and I'm on my way to try them out. Please excuse me." Still another said, "I have just got married, so I can't come"' (Luke 14:16–20). I am not going to talk about the first and last excuses, but just about the one who bought five yoke of oxen, as he will help us in our understanding here. The five yoke of oxen stand for your five senses which have the animal instincts of the wild oxen. The man was not rejected from the banquet because he had bought the five yoke of oxen but because he went to try them out and so would not come to the banquet. In the same way it is not wrong to use your senses in the way they were intended. What is wrong is for you to indulge yourself in the use of your senses. If you do this to the extent that you are fully taken up with your senses and completely satisfied by them, then you have committed a deadly sin. You have chosen your senses to be your god and so you are excluded from the banquet. St Paul teaches us not to use our senses in this way when he says we are not to 'gratify the desires of the sinful nature' (Gal. 5:16). I trust that you are not caught up in such a deadly sin, as it is so difficult to escape from.

So long as you set your heart on loving God and receiving his grace you will only commit a venial sin when you give in to your senses. You are not giving yourself over to them completely and rejecting God in the process. You will not be excluded from the banquet on account of your venial sins. But you will lose the joy of experiencing the delights of the banquet on earth. But you can change this by using all your strength to defeat your venial sins. Then you will find that your spiritual desires grow.

You may object that you cannot stop hearing about the selfish way of life from the people who live in the world.

My reply is that you should not be hurt from speaking with your neighbours, but helped from such conversations if you act wisely. You will be able to discover the extent of your love. Your duty is to love your neighbour from the heart, and this includes doing anything he asks so long as it is reasonable. However, you are not able to assist your neighbour by leaving your enclosed order. But, you can be loving in your heart towards your neighbour. When a neighbour comes to talk with you, give yourself totally to this meeting. Act as if you were an angel who had come to speak. Find out what the person needs and wants to say. If you are praying and your neighbour arrives to talk with you, you should speak with him at once. You are not leaving God behind. You should bring God with you as you speak so that you only see God and hear God in your conversation with your neighbour.

It will do you no harm at all to speak discreetly with a neighbour. You should gently ask the neighbour why he has come to speak with you. He may have come to unburden himself to you about some trouble so that he can be comforted by you. If so, you should listen to him carefully and allow him to speak as he wants to. You should then comfort him gently and lovingly and then stop. If he continues and passes on idle gossip, do not reply to him or encourage him in any way. He will soon become tired of this and will leave.

If someone arrives in order to teach you, listen to him humbly out of respect for his order. If you are encouraged by what he says, you can ask him to help you further. Do not try to teach him, because it is not your job to teach priests, except when it is absolutely necessary. If you are not helped by what he says, do not say much in reply and he will soon leave.

If somebody else comes to you to give you money or else to learn from you, speak to him gently and humbly. Do not reprove anybody for his faults, because that is not your job unless the person is well known to you and you know that he will take the rebuke from you. Be brief with any rebuke that you give. If you think that he will benefit from such a rebuke, then you should go ahead and rebuke him. The most important thing to remember when you are speaking with a neighbour is that you should speak as little as possible. Then you will find that your devotions will be interrupted as little as possible. I am giving you my opinion here. If you can do better than this, do so.

10

THREE KINDS OF PEOPLE

You may think that just because you are a member of an enclosed religious order that you have closed the windows of your five senses. You may think that you only use your senses for the sake of necessity. My reply to this is that if you have succeeded in doing this you have then indeed closed a big window on your sinful image. However, this does not make you safe. You have not yet managed to block up all the holes which are formed through the thoughts that come into your mind. You may be able to picture me in your mind even if I am not present with you in my body. This is true of all bodily things. So if you let your soul feed on worldly desires that are in your mind, your soul is outside your enclosed order even when your body remains shut up inside.

Now you ask me if it matters that a soul is preoccupied in its mind with outward senses or inner thoughts. My reply is that this question should never be asked in the first place. Anybody who genuinely loves God should not be enquiring whether one sin is greater than another sin. People must realise that whatever sin keeps them from God is a serious sin. Everything is sinful that is not good and stops you from loving God. What is sin if it is not a lack of goodness? You must run away from all sins, whether they are deadly or venial.

11

SUMMARY

From what I have said you will have a good idea about the darkness of the image of sin. I have not told you everything about this, for that would be impossible. But from what I have said you will be able to see this image more clearly.

You may wonder how I know that you have such an image in you. My answer comes from the prophet who said: 'I have found an idol in myself' (Hos. 12:8, Vulgate). This is a false image, evil and disfigured by the sins I have mentioned. Through these sins I am thrown into sensual pleasure, and away from purity of heart and delight in spiritual matters. I am greatly upset by this fall of mine and I cry out to God for his mercy. Because I feel my own wretchedness so strongly I am able to talk to you about your own image. We are all descended from Adam and Eve and clothed in animal skins, as the Bible says: 'The Lord God made garments of skin for Adam and his wife and clothed them' (Gen. 3:21). This clothing made from animals accurately reflects the sinful state in which we have fallen and the spiritual condition we are now in.

The image is an ugly one. Its head is pride. For pride is the first sin, as the wise man has said: 'The beginning of all manner of sin is pride' (Ecclus. 10:15, Vulgate). Covetousness forms the rear part of the image. As St Paul says: 'Forgetting what is behind and straining towards what is ahead, I press on towards the goal to win the prize' (Phil. 3:13–14). Paul is talking about leaving all worldly things behind him. Envy is the heart of the image. It is not a selfish sin, for it comes from the devil. As the wise man says: 'Death came into the world only through the Devil's envy' (Wisd. 2:14, NJB). Everybody who belongs to the devil follows him into this den of envy. Anger forms the arms of the image. People express their anger through their arms. As the gospel says: 'If someone strikes you on the right cheek,' you should not hit him back, but 'turn to him the other also' (Matt. 5:39). Greed is the image's stomach. As St Paul says: '"Food for the stomach and the stomach for food" – but God will destroy them both' (1 Cor. 6:13). This will happen on judgement day, when the chosen will complete their reformation and the reprobate be damned. Lust is part of your body, as St Paul says: 'Do not offer the parts of your body to sin, as instruments of wickedness' (Rom. 6:13). This applies particularly to the sin of lust. The image's feet are laziness. So the wise man said to the lazy person, trying to stir him to do good deeds: 'Do this now, my son, and deliver thyself' (Prov. 6:3, AV). Encourage your friend to start doing good deeds, which are prayer and devotion to Jesus. These are the different parts of the image.

12

YOUR IMAGE AND JESUS' IMAGE

The image I have just described is not the image of Jesus, for it is more like the image of the devil. The image of Jesus is made up of the virtues of Christian love and humility. The image I described in the last chapter is made up of a false love of yourself, with all the parts of it attached to that love. You bear the mark of this on you, as does everybody else in the world until they have it destroyed by the grace of Jesus. David appears to be talking about this in the Psalms: 'Man is a mere phantom as he goes to and fro: He bustles about, but only in vain' (Ps. 39:6). It is as if he is saying that although man was created firmly in the image of God, he has become unstable because he sinned and is living in the world. St Paul speaks about this image: 'Just as we have borne the likeness of the earthly man, so shall we bear the likeness of the man from heaven' (1 Cor. 15:49).

What are you to do about your sinful image? I reply in the words the Jews used to tell Pilate what to do to Christ, 'Crucify him.' Take your body of sin and crucify it. Break this image of sin and kill this false love of sin in yourself. Just as Christ's body was broken for our sins, so it is right if you want to be like Christ for you to put to death your selfish lusts. St Paul wrote: 'Those who belong to Christ

Jesus have crucified the sinful nature with its passions and desires' (Gal. 5:24). Kill off your pride and set up humility in its place. Pull down anger and envy and replace them with love towards God and love for your neighbour. Substitute being poor in spirit for covetousness. Instead of being lazy be keen to perform good deeds. Replace your greed and lust with sobriety and love in your body and your soul. This is advised by St Paul: 'You were taught, with regard to your former way of life, to put off your old self, which is being corrupted by its deceitful desires; to be made new in the attitude of your minds; and to put on the new self, created to be like God in true righteousness and holiness' (Eph. 4:22–24). Who is going to help you destroy your sinful image? Truly it will only be the Lord Jesus. If you pray to him about this idol of yours with all your heart, he will help you.

In your heart follow the advice of the wise man: 'Above all else, guard your heart, for it is the wellspring of life' (Prov. 4:23). Your heart is protected when wise thoughts, pure emotions and a strong desire to be loving surround it. Then a soul lives a blissfully happy life endued with heavenly blessing. But if your heart is left unguarded it becomes like the heart our Lord described in the gospels: 'For out of the heart come evil thoughts, murder, adultery, sexual immorality, theft, false testimony, slander. These are what make a man "unclean"' (Matt. 15:19–20). In this way the soul is either killed by deadly sins or numbed by venial sins. For what is a man if he is not his thoughts and desires? They alone make a man good or bad. The state of your soul is dependent on how much you love God and love your neighbour and know God. If you only love God in a small way, your soul will be tiny. And if you do not love God at all, your soul is nothing. It is nothing as far as good is concerned, but it is great as far as sin is concerned. If you want to know where the centre of your love is, work out what you think about most. Your love is where your longing is. If you love God a lot you will think about him a lot, and if you do not love God much you will rarely think about him. If you defeat your thoughts and emotions, you will become virtuous.

You must break down this image once you appreciate your inner wretchedness and your own pride, envy, vanity and covetousness. You are full of corruption. You are slow to sense God and spiritual things but quick to delight in earthly things. You are full of sin as a hide is full of meat. But you must not become depressed as you think about yourself in this way. Rather, you must turn your attention to the Lord Jesus, pray for his help, and call to him with deep longing in your heart that he will either help you to bear this great burden or else will break the image for you. Remember how shameful it is for you to eat pig's food when you should be experiencing heavenly joy.

If you do as I have said, you will begin to oppose the foundation of sin in you. This experience may cause you pain and sorrow. You need to know that no soul can live without pain, heaviness and sorrow unless she rests in or delights in her Creator or in a created person. So you will feel pain as you seek to experience the Lord Jesus within you and as you move away from your love of all bodily feelings. You will find that you become a burden to yourself and it will feel as if everybody is against you and that everything that once gave you pleasure now becomes a burden. Once you have forsaken all these things, and before your soul finds comfort from God, you will experience pain. You must, however, be steadfast as you endure this suffering, clinging to the single desire of knowing only Jesus Christ. Do not look for any outward comforts at this time. Your suffering will not last long, as our Lord is near to you. Our Lord will comfort you and will help you to cope with your corrupt human nature. Through his merciful and gracious presence he will break down your false image of love. This will not happen all at once, but little by little, until the image of the Lord Jesus begins to be formed in you.

Once you have defeated yourself so comprehensively you will be able to govern yourself more easily. With greater love you will be able to protect your thoughts and emotions and you will be able to see whether they are good or bad. So if, for example, you feel pride welling up in you, you will not allow it to escape lightly. You will take it in hand and tear it to pieces. You will not give it any room to speak its lies, because you know that its engaging tones have nothing to do with the truth. As the prophet has said: 'O my people, your guides lead you astray; they turn you from the path' (Isa. 3:12).

If you are diligent about this you will, through the grace of Jesus, soon stop the spring of pride in you so that you no longer take delight in being proud. When you do feel pride stirring in you, it will be so weak that it will feel as if it was half dead, and it will not be much trouble to you. Then you will have the spiritual sight to view the virtue of humility. You will see how good and attractive it is and how much you desire and love it. Then you will be happy to look at yourself and for other people to see you as you are. For you are full of corruption which you suffer happily out of your love for righteousness.

Be alert to resist the first sign of anger or ill-will against your neighbour, no matter how justified you think it may be. Do not encourage it by word or deed, but kill it out of reverence for God. These feelings of pride, vanity, envy and other sins will rise in your heart, but they will not upset you if you steadfastly resist them with your will and mind. Do not worry that these feelings stay in your heart, because although they may rob you of your peace they do not defile you.

You must deal with the first evil signs of covetousness, laziness, greed and lechery in the same way. Be prepared to defeat them with your mind and your will.

You will be able to succeed in this if you set your heart on nothing other than God. Long to please him, know him and love him. Desire to experience his grace in part now and in full measure in heaven. If your desire to know God remains strong, you will be able to distinguish between what is sin and what is not sin, and between what is good and what is best. If you cling to your desire to know God, you will learn everything you need to know and have everything you want. When you are fighting against the foundation of sin in general, or against any particular sin, focus on God whom you desire rather than on the sin itself which you hate. When you do this God fights on your side and he will destroy sin in you. You will be successful in this much more quickly when you set your heart on God than when you concentrate on the rising sin. You will never destroy sin through your own efforts.

13

FORMING THE IMAGE OF CHRIST IN YOU

Do what I have told you, and more if you can, and I know that through the grace of Jesus you will shame the devil and break down all his evil desires which trouble you so much. This is how you are to break down and destroy your image of sin which deforms you and changes you from the image of Christ. Then you will be remoulded into the image of the humanity of Jesus, through humility and love. Later you will conform to the image of the Godhead itself. On earth, as you contemplate, this is like a shadow, but in heaven you will experience the reality of this.

St Paul speaks about conforming to the likeness of Christ: 'My dear children, for whom I am again in the pains of childbirth until Christ is formed in you' (Gal. 4:19). Christ was conceived in you through faith. Christ lives in your soul through grace to the extent that you wish to serve him and please him. But Christ is not fully formed in you, and you are not fully formed in Christ through complete love. So St Paul goes through the pains of childbirth for you and me until Christ is fully formed in us and we in him.

14

CONCLUSION

Anybody who thinks that he can contemplate properly, except through the perfection of virtues, is not entering by the door but is a thief and must be thrown out. I am not denying that many people may have a taste of the contemplative life from time to time. Some people experience this at their conversion. But they will not have this as their permanent experience until some virtues have been perfected in them. Christ is both the door and the doorkeeper, and nobody can enter without his permission. Jesus said: 'No-one comes to the Father except through me' (John 14:6). Nobody can come to the contemplation of the Godhead unless he is first transfigured through humility and love into the likeness of Jesus' humanity.

So I have now told you a little about the contemplative life and how to attain it through God's grace. I can talk about this although I have not experienced it fully myself. Nevertheless, through this writing, I remind myself about my own negligence in this area and resolve to improve. I also hope to stir up you and other men and women who have entered into seeking the contemplative life. May they work more diligently and more humbly in this way of life through these simple words which were given to me through the grace of God. If you find anything in what I have written that encourages you to love God more, give thanks to God because it is his gift and not the words that I have written. If you are not comforted by what I have written, or if you do not quickly understand it, do not spend a long time studying it, put it to one side for another time. Carry on praying and going about your business. Read what I have written as you are able, and not all at once.

Do not be bound by what I have written. If on reflection you think that I have made mistakes through faulty reasoning or faulty writing, then correct them as necessary. What I have written applies not to people who lead a life of activity, but to those who are seeking to live the contemplative life.

The grace of our Lord Jesus Christ be with you.